THIRD EDITION

SOVIET NAVAL DEVELOPMENTS

THIRD EDITION

SOVIET NAVAL DEVELOPMENTS

Based on a Report
Prepared at the direction of the
Chief of Naval Operations by the
Director of Naval Intelligence
and Chief of Information

Department of the Navy, Washington, D.C.

Foreword by NORMAN POLMAR

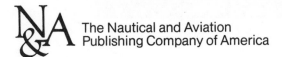
The Nautical and Aviation
Publishing Company of America

Library of Congress Cataloging in Publication Data
Main entry under title:

Soviet naval developments.

    1. Soviet Union. Voenno-Morskoi flot.
2. Merchant marine--Soviet Union. 3. Sea-power
--Soviet Union. I. United States. Office of
Naval Intelligence. II. United States. Navy
Dept. Office of the Chief of Information.
VA573.S567 1984   359® .00947   81-14104
ISBN 0-933852-44-4   AACR2

Library of Congress Catalog Card Number: 81 14104
ISBN 0-933852-44-4
Printed in the United States of America

Foreword

The Soviet Union continues in the 1980s to expend considerable resources to increase its naval as well as related maritime and industrial capabilities. This can be seen most dramatically in the continued introduction and series production of new ship classes. No less than four classes of modern cruisers and destroyers (one nuclear powered) and ten classes of submarines (seven nuclear powered) are being built in Soviet shipyards. At the same time, the last of the four KIEV-class Vertical Take-Off and Landing (VTOL) aircraft carriers is being completed while a larger, nuclear-powered carrier has been started.

Coupled with this impressive development of new ships, the Soviet Navy has kept pace with advances in component weapons and sensors, surveillance and targeting systems, and command and control structure.

As this new "hardware" is being developed the Soviet Navy has kept up the relatively high tempo of operations that began in the 1960s until today the U.S. and Soviet fleets maintain approximately the same number of "ship days" of naval units out of their respective coastal areas. (This is exclusive of strategic missile submarines; the U.S. Navy maintains a much higher fraction of its force at sea.)

The chief architect of this fleet is Admiral of the Fleet of the Soviet Union S.G. Gorshkov, who became CINC of the Soviet Navy in January 1956. An astute politician as well as executive, Gorshkov has stressed advanced technologies and operations while at the same time maintaining a large number of ships and submarines in active commission. While rumors persist of his stepping down, at age 73 he appears to be in full command. However, certain non-naval developments in the Soviet Union could lead to a slowdown of the rate of naval development in the near future. The death of L.I. Brezhnev in November 1982 appears to have ended the close ties that Gorshkov enjoyed with the chief of state and first party secretary. There seems to be no similar relationship with Brezhnev's successors. At the same time, there are continuing demands from the four other Soviet armed forces—the Strategic Rocket Forces, Air Defense Forces, Ground Forces, and Air Forces—for more resources to modernize their forces, to help counter the U.S. defense buildup being sponsored by the Reagan Administration.

Thus, the programs described in this volume may become increasingly controversial within the Kremlin, and Admiral Gorshkov and his eventual successors will have more of a battle on their hands to continue to receive the material resources, industrial capacity, and trained personnel that the modern Soviet fleet demands.

This volume seeks to provide a brief overview of these Soviet naval developments. The idea for this work originated a decade ago, in discussions with the U.S. Navy's Director of Naval Intelligence and the Chief of Information as a means of providing U.S. naval officers with an unclassified synopsis of Soviet activities. The first edition was published by the U.S. Navy in 1974; subsequently it has been published in revised editions by the Navy. The widespread demand for the volume led to the U.S. Government Printing Office undertaking a soft-cover edition and commercial publication of a hard-bound edition by the Nautical & Aviation Publishing Company. This edition is based on the U.S. Navy's Third Edition, which has been extensively updated by the staff of Nautical & Aviation.

Norman Polmar
November 1, 1983

Table of Contents

Section 1. Purpose

The Soviet Navy has been transformed into an important strategic force, into a force capable of opposing aggression from the sea and accomplishing major operational and strategic missions on the World Ocean. . . . Its relative weight within the composition of the (Soviet) armed forces is continually increasing. . . .

Admiral of the Fleet of the Soviet Union
S.G. GORSHKOV

One of the most dramatic developments of the post-World War II period has been the growth of Soviet naval and maritime activities.* Today the Soviet Union is a true "sea power" challenging United States in all aspects of maritime activity. From the end of World War II until the early 1970s the United States maintained unquestioned naval supremacy. This gave the United States great flexibility in foreign policy and provided one of the West's primary shields against Soviet aggression.

During much of this period the Soviet Navy—except for submarines—was ranked fourth after the U.S., British, and French navies. Only in numbers of submarines could the Soviet Navy rank as a leader at sea in the early post-war era, reaching a peak of some 450 diesel submarines in 1958. Although the Soviet Navy had quantitative superiority in undersea craft, there were substantial qualitative shortcomings in equipment, personnel, and leadership. Further, Soviet surface warships and submarines seldom ventured far from the coasts of the U.S.S.R.

Today, after a great expenditure of resources, the Soviet Navy has achieved quantitative and qualitative leadership is several aspects of naval power. This Soviet leadership, both real and perceived, is having considerable impact on international political, economic, ideological, and military developments.

Accordingly, it is important for U.S. Navy personnel to be professionally knowledgeable about the Soviet Navy and its development. Further, it is not enough that just we in the Navy understand Soviet naval developments. We must also assist in illuminating the issues for the American public about this unprecedented peacetime expansion of naval power. This Fourth Edition of *Understanding Soviet Naval Developments* is intended to provide the necessary background information for naval personnel to discuss the Soviet Navy intelligently both internally and in public forums.

There is a tendency in some quarters to foster scenarios which place the Soviet Navy in the best light while placing the U.S. Navy in "worst case" situations. This approach is alarmist and misleading, just as the position that all Soviet naval developments are strictly defensive or are merely a reaction to U.S. and other NATO actions, is complacent and misleading. The Soviet Navy is inferior in several important respects to the U.S. Navy; it has problems and limitations as has the military service of any nation. These will be discussed later in the text.

The considerable influence that the Soviet Navy exerts in world affairs today can be traced to the great strides that it has made in technology, production, operations, and tactics, as well as its extensive use as an instrument of Soviet foreign policy. These developments are of major concern to the U.S. Navy because they narrow the options open to the United States in a crisis situation, and because they could result in confrontations with the Soviet Navy or with other navies which employ Soviet weapons and tactics.

This publication discusses the expansion of Soviet maritime strength from its beginnings to its present status and the trends which are indicated for the future. The manual has been published for the widest dissemination within the Navy.

In this context, "maritime activities" includes the merchant marine, fishing industry, research and shipbuilding activities.

The Tsarist Russian battleship RETVIZAN's visit to New York in 1901 gave Americans one of their few looks at Russian naval forces. Some American perceptions of Russian naval developments may date back to the RETVIZAN and her participation in the Russo-Japanese War of 1904–1905, a Russian disaster. In the foreground is the U.S. submarine HOLLAND.

The nuclear powered missile cruiser KIROV is a symbol of the rash of new classes of warships and submarines which the Soviets will be adding to their fleet in the decade of the eighties—larger with more sophisticated weapons and sensors than their impressive predecessors. KIROV is the Soviets' first nuclear powered warship and is the largest warship (less carriers) built by any navy since the end of World War II.

Section 2. Soviet Naval Policy

The flag of the Soviet Navy flies over the oceans of the world. Sooner or later the United States will have to understand it no longer has mastery of the seas.

Admiral of the Fleet of the Soviet Union
S.G. GORSHKOV

Soviet naval policy is based on a Russian drive to extend national influence by maritime activities, a drive which dates back almost 300 years. This effort has continued, with varying emphasis, under the Tsars, and the commissars who followed them. Sometimes spearheaded by explorers and researchers, at times by the merchant fishing fleets, often by the navy, this effort is now being made by a combination of all of these maritime forces on a scale without precedent.

A. Perspective, 1700–1953

The Soviet Navy traces its beginnings from the early 1700s when the Western-oriented Tsar Peter I founded a city (now Leningrad) on the Neva marshes at the eastern end of the Gulf of Finland and built a navy to fight the Swedes. Prior to that time the only secure Russion outlet to the sea was on the frigid Arctic coast. Employing British and Dutch shipbuilders and officers, Peter constructed a fleet which achieved major victories against the enemy, and established Russia as a power in the Baltic region. Later, America's naval hero of the Revolution, John Paul Jones, served as an admiral in the Russian Navy during the reign of Catherine the Great.

During the centuries that followed, Tsarist, and then Soviet, naval forces had few victories at sea of which to boast. Although there were some decisive triumphs against the Turks in the 18th and 19th centuries, British and French naval forces present in the Mediterranean and elsewhere, frustrated Russian ambitions.

The overwhelming defeats inflicted on Russian fleets by the Japanese Navy in the war of 1904–1905 dramatically demonstrated the former's shortcomings—a lack of preparedness, poor coordination, and an inability to sustain prolonged operations on the high seas far from home ports. A decade later, in World War I, the Russian Navy was ineffective in the conflict against Germany, a cause for disillusionment among the sailors who later became the torchbearers of the second, or Bolshevik, revolution in the fall of 1917.

The revolutions and the civil war that followed had destroyed the navy and other maritime resources, including shipbuilding. Among other things, the "torchbearer" sailors, whose cooperation had been crucial to the success of the Bolshevik revolution, turned against the government in an open revolt at Kronshtadt in March 1921 demanding an end to Communist Party dictatorship, political freedom and civil rights. Needless to say, the Soviet authorities put down the revolt by shooting some of the former heroes and imprisoning others. Yet today, this nasty incident is all but forgotten and the men of the Navy are held in high esteem by the Soviet government.

Not until extensive shipyard expansion in the early 1930s could the Soviets begin construction of large submarines and destroyers. Although several cruisers and battleships were begun on the eve of World War II, only a few were completed and those that were available contributed little to the outcome of the conflict.

Interestingly enough, the way having been paved for World War II by a hastily concluded Soviet-German friendship pact, the Soviets had the world's largest submarine fleet. There were 165 Soviet submarines compared to 57 in the German Navy, and 95 in the U.S. Navy. When the Soviet Union entered the war in June 1941 they had 218 submarines. Yet these undersea craft enjoyed few successes, and had no impact on the course of the war due to geographic limitations and climatic conditions which often left them ice-bound in the Baltic. Poor training, outmoded tactics, and an inability to cope with German mines and other antisubmarine forces further neutralized the Soviet undersea fleet. Thus, the Soviet Navy played only a minor, supporting role in the conflict. It was the massive Soviet Army which won the great battles that contributed significantly to the defeat of Hitler's Germany. And it was the Army which remained as the Soviet Union's threat to the war-ravaged nations of Eastern and Western Europe after the war had ended. As peace came the Soviet Union again was incapable of building a major fleet; one-third of the country had been overrun by German armies and 20 million persons—ten percent of the population—had either been killed in battle or had died of privation.

Still, Joseph Stalin, the Soviet dictator, sought an ocean-going navy for the Soviet Union. High priorities were given to this task and by the late 1940s, the nation's shipbuilding industry had been rebuilt sufficiently (in part by using German technology and engineers) to begin work on submarines, battleships, cruisers and destroyers. Even construction of aircraft carriers was planned, but Stalin died in March 1953 and his schemes for an oceangoing fleet were buried with him. In the months that followed the dictator's death, shipbuilding programs were cancelled or cut back. For example, only 14 of 24 projected SVERDLOV class light cruisers were completed; none of the larger STALINGRAD class cruisers or pre-war SOVIET UNION class battleships was finished and the carrier program did not get past the drawing board.

B. Khrushchev's Policies

Nikita Khrushchev, when he emerged as the new ruler of the Kremlin, initiated new policies affecting the size and composition of the Soviet Navy. In 1956, he appointed Sergei Gorshkov, a 45 year-old naval officer who had attained the rank of rear admiral at the age of 31 to be Commander-in-Chief of the Soviet Navy and directed him to dismantle the larger surface warships. Khrushchev's point-of-view in this regard, is reflected in a remark attributed to him that large warships were only useful for hauling around admirals. As a consequence, Admiral Gorshkov presided over the dismantling of much of Stalin's big-ship navy. Existing battleships were scrapped, as were several older cruisers and destroyers. Many personnel were either retired or dismissed; and all of the several thousand land-based fighter aircraft of the Soviet Navy were transferred to the National Air Defense Forces.**

In the place of Stalin's planned ocean-going fleet,

Admiral Gorshkov was directed to develop a missile-armed navy of small craft and submarines which could "defend the Soviet Union from possible Western aggression." It was hoped that comparatively inexpensive guided (cruise) missiles could counter the U.S. naval forces which were then being augmented during the Korean War (1950–1953). Soviet military planners were particularly concerned with U.S. aircraft carriers which could launch planes carrying nuclear bombs against their homeland while several hundred miles at sea, and with amphibious forces which could land troops on the Soviet coasts.

During the 1950s the Soviet Navy developed destroyers and submarines that could fire against U.S. aircraft carriers while the Soviet ships remained under the protection of land-based fighter aircraft. For coastal defense, the Soviets built the famed KOMAR and then OSA classes of missile boats which were armed with STYX (SS-N-2) antiship missiles. Also, several hundred medium bombers were transferred to Soviet Naval Aviation for use against ships and submarines.

By the late 1950s Admiral Gorshkov was able to obtain approval for larger missile-firing ships. The first of these were the KYNDA class cruisers. Each has eight launching tubes plus eight reloads for the SS-N-3 antiship missile. With target acquisition provided by either an aircraft, a submarine, or a surface ship, the missile can deliver up to a ton of high explosives or a nuclear warhead against hostile ships some 250 miles away.

This concern for countering aircraft carriers was intense during the 1950s and 1960s and substantial resources were dedicated to this task. Although in recent years the strategic missile submarine force and antisubmarine warfare (ASW) received greater emphasis, the Soviet Navy still maintains extensive and formidable anticarrier forces. The latest weapon system assigned to this task is the supersonic BACKFIRE bomber, and several new missile and ship designs appear to be primarily intended for the antiship role.

Soviet concern about the U.S. Navy, centered on the strategic striking power of carrier-based aircraft, assumed a new dimension in 1960 when the first U.S. ballistic missile submarine, GEORGE WASHINGTON, went to sea carrying 16 POLARIS strategic missiles. Forty-one U.S. nuclear powered,

---

**Since 1960 the Soviet Union has had five separate military services or forces. In their normal order of precedence they are: Strategic Rocket Forces, Ground Forces, National Air Defense Forces; Air Forces and Navy.*

ballistic missile submarines were completed from 1960 to 1967, providing a massive deterrent to Soviet aggression. Later, most of these submarines were converted to carry the longer range POSEIDON missile and twelve of these submarines are presently being back-fitted with the 4,000 mile range TRIDENT I weapon.

Response by the Soviet Navy to U.S. strategic missile submarines included construction of new classes of antisubmarine ships, among them the unusual and unique helicopter carrying missile cruisers MOSKVA and LENINGRAD. These well armed ships, described in detail in a subsequent section, each operate up to 18 ASW helicopters fitted with submarine detection devices and capable of carrying bombs or torpedoes.

The Soviet Navy under Khrushchev thus was configured as an aggressively employed defensive force, initially used for close-in coastal defense, then to attack approaching U.S. aircraft carriers and then to counter the threat from strategic missile submarines.

However, the ships, submarines and aircraft developed for these roles would be capable of carrying out other Soviet military objectives, as well as supporting political and even economic goals, particularly in peacetime. Like large navies before it, the modern Soviet fleet would prove to be a highly flexible instrument for use by that nation's leadership.

C. The Navy Goes To Sea

Admiral Gorshkov only partially implemented Khrushchev's directives to halt big-ship building programs and dispose of many older warships. In point of fact, 14 of the SVERDLOV class light cruisers were completed during this period of upheaval. It would only be a few years later that Gorshkov, unhindered by directives to the contrary, had the Soviet Navy building large surface war ships. In the interim he pushed development of missile-armed destroyers, patrol boats and diesel submarines, as

Perhaps the most impressive manifestation of the Soviet Navy's current thrust are the KIEV class VTOL aircraft carriers. Although of limited capability in comparison with U.S. Navy carriers, these four ships still demonstrate the huge allocation of resources to the Soviet Navy and the advances being made.

well as nuclear powered submarines. The first of these new ships appeared in the late 1950s.

Still, Admiral Gorshkov was unable to build an ocean-going fleet except for the aforementioned submarines, and even there the Soviet Navy had operational limitations. The lack of a far-ranging fleet was politically embarrassing to the Soviet government in 1956 when Anglo-French naval forces invaded Suez, in 1958 when U.S. naval forces landed in Lebanon and in 1962 when a U.S. naval blockade (and the threat of overwhelming nuclear retaliation) forced the Soviets to withdraw strategic weapons from Cuba. In these situations the Soviets virtually had no options for countering Western political-military activities at sea except by propaganda. These lessons appear to have indelibly impressed the present leaders in the Kremlin.

In 1963 the Soviet Navy Chief "ordered his men to sea." Despite limitations in training, experience, support capabilities and the like, the Soviet Navy began operating beyond its traditional coastal areas and out of its defensive posture. By mid-1964 Soviet warships had established a continual presence in the Mediterranean. An average of five ships were maintained in the Mediterranean that year; the number gradually increased and soon Mediterranean port visits were scheduled. During the Arab-Israeli war in June 1967, a steady stream of Soviet ships passed through the Turkish Straits into the Mediterranean until the Soviet Mediterranean Squadron numbered about 70 surface warships, submarines, and support ships.

Subsequently, the Soviet Navy has maintained an average of at least 40 to 45 ships in the Mediterranean. Periodically, the number increases as relieving surface ships from the Black Sea Fleet and submarines from the Northern Fleet enter the Mediterranean (through the Strait of Gibraltar) and operate for a short period of time together with the ships they are replacing.

Soviet ability to rapidly deploy naval forces in the Mediterranean area was demonstrated in October-November 1973. Within a few days of the outbreak of hostilities in the Middle East, a steady stream of Soviet naval ships passed south through the Turkish Straits, and a second Northern Fleet submarine group entered the Mediterranean. These forces doubled the strength of the Soviet Mediterranean Squadron.

By early November, when the 1973 crisis reached its peak, there were 96 Soviet naval units in the Mediterranean: 5 cruisers, 14 destroyers, 6 patrol ships, 2 NANUCHKA class middle ships, 9 amphibious ships, 6 intelligence ships, and approxi-mately 25 submarines (several of which were nuclear-powered); with the remainder being nearly 30 support ships. The surface ships had 20 surface-to-air missile launchers as well as a considerable number of antiship missiles. Several of the submarines also carried antiship missiles.

However, neither one of the two MOSKVA class helicopter carriers was in the Mediterranean, nor was the new KARA class cruiser NIKOLAYEV, which had left the Mediterranean on the eve of the buildup. The absence of these ships indicated that the powerful and unprecedented reinforcement of the Soviet Mediterranean Squadron was less than an all-out effort. Possibly the Soviet strategy called for withholding these primarily ASW ships at the beginning of a conflict, or they simply did not wish to risk these high-value ships in the Middle East conflict.

Still, the Soviets were able to deploy 96 surface ships and submarines into the Mediterranean during a period when the U.S. Sixth Fleet reached a peak strength of 66 ships. The three aircraft carriers then present provided the most potent U.S. conventional warfare capabilities in the region. Although Soviet Black Sea Fleet naval aircraft were within striking range of the eastern Mediterranean, they would have had to violate Turkish air-space to get there.

The only other strike aircraft in the immediate area at the time which could have been made available to the Soviets were 12 TU-22 BLINDER bombers recently delivered to Iraq. However, airfields in Egypt and Libya (including the former U.S. Wheelus Air Force Base) had, in the past, supported Soviet aircraft and could have accommodated Soviet BADGERs and BLINDERs if political permission were obtained.

In addition to the naval buildup, it is interesting to observe that very shortly after hostilities erupted between Israel and the Arab states, numerous Soviet merchant ships began loading tanks, aircraft and other war material in Black Sea ports. Most of the estimated 2,000 tanks that were supplied to the Arab armies after the outbreak of war, as well as considerable amounts of other war supplies, were transported to Egypt and Syria by Soviet merchant ships. These ships complemented the intensive Soviet airlift delivering more time-critical items such as disassembled fighter aircraft and guided missiles.

Soviet warships began operating regularly in the Indian Ocean during the late 1960s, in the Caribbean in 1969 and off the western coast of Africa late in 1970. The Kremlin leadership had discovered Sea Power!

These warships, flying the Soviet Hammer and

Admiral of the Fleet of the Soviet Union Sergey Georgiyevich Gorshkov has been the Commander-in-Chief of the Soviet Navy since 1956. Under his leadership the navy has been transformed from a coastal defense force into a formidable global strategic force which is now a flexible instrument of Soviet foreign policy. A Great Russian born 26 February 1910, Gorshkov joined the navy in 1927, after graduation from Frunze Higher Naval School. He served in destroyers in the Black Sea and Pacific Fleets through the 1930s and was appointed Rear Admiral in 1941—right after the Germans declared war on the U.S.S.R. He distinguished himself in several Black Sea commands during the war including the Azov and Danube Flotillas. He was commander of the Black Sea Fleet when he was picked for the Commander-in-Chief. Gorshkov also is a Deputy Minister of Defense and a Full Member of the Central Committee of the Communist Party. His "hats" make him the approximate equivalent of both the Secretary of Navy, a civilian position, and the Chief of Naval Operations in the U.S. Navy organization. Gorshkov has published a number of works; best known are his series of articles entitled *Navies in War and Peace* and his widely distributed book, *The Sea Power of the State*, now in its second edition.

Sickle, represent Soviet interests—economic, political and military. The Soviets are employing their navy in much the same way as the United States, Great Britain and other naval powers effectively used ships to support their national interests in various parts of the world during the previous decades. In their rediscovery of the use of ships to support state interests, the capabilities of the Soviet Navy have expanded greatly, and the tasks and missions assigned to the Navy also have increased in scope and number.

D. Expanding Naval Missions

Over the last two decades the Soviet Navy has been transformed from a basically coastal defense force into an ocean-going fleet designed to extend the defenses of the U.S.S.R. well to sea, and to perform most of the traditional functions of a naval power in waters distant from the Soviet Union. Multi-ocean exercises, such as OKEAN-70 and 75, and the continued naval presence in distant seas, supported by the construction of larger, more powerful warships manifest this evolution of the role of the Soviet Navy in world affairs.

Recent Soviet military writings also reflect the evolution of naval missions. An example of this is the 1976 article on the Soviet Navy signed by Admiral Gorshkov in the *Soviet Military Encyclopedia*, which characterized the Navy as:

> *The branch of the armed forces intended to carry out strategic and operational missions in the sea and ocean theaters of combat operations. With respect to its combat capabilities, today's Navy is capable of delivering strikes by its strategic nuclear forces against important enemy ground targets, of destroying his naval forces at sea and in their bases, of disrupting enemy ocean and sea communications and protecting our own sea communications, and to evacuate the sick and wounded. The navy can conduct a naval operation both independently and jointly with other branches of the armed forces.*

By studying such writings of Soviet authors, particularly Admiral Gorshkov's most recent book *Sea Power of the State* (2nd ed., revised 1978), by analyzing Soviet naval exercises and activity and by observing the ships, aircraft and weapons built by the Soviets, a reasonable understanding of their naval missions can be determined.

According to Admiral Gorshkov, the basic mission of the Soviet Navy is the "battle against the shore." He writes that:

> *In our day, a navy operating against the*

shore possessed the capability . . . of directly affecting the course and even the outcome of the war. In this connection, naval operations against the shore have assumed dominant importance in naval warfare, and both the technical policy of building a navy and the development of the art of naval warfare have been subordinated to them.

The "battle against the shore" is used in both the offensive and defensive sense, and includes strategic missile strikes against enemy "shore" targets, attacking the enemy's threat to one's own "shore," and supporting the ground forces. More specifically, Soviet naval missions can be stated as: (1) strategic offense, (2) maritime security of the Soviet Union, (3) interdiction of sea lines of communication, (4) support of the ground forces and, in situations short of general war, (5) the support of state policy.

Strategic Offensive

The priority given to the development of ballistic missile submarines (SSBN) since the early 1960s makes it clear that strategic nuclear strike has become a prime mission of the Soviet Navy. From 1967 to 1983 Soviet shipyards completed 70 nuclear-powered strategic missile submarines of the YANKEE and DELTA classes.

Construction of the large DELTA III submarines is continuing while the initial unit of the much-larger TYPHOON class was completed in 1983. This submarine displaces some 25,000 tons submerged and carries 20 very large SS-N-20 ballistic missiles. By comparison, the U.S. OHIO-class submarines displace 18,700 tons submerged and carry 24 TRIDENT Submarine-Launched Ballistic Missiles (SLBMs).

Accompanying this intensive strategic submarine program has been a succession of improved SLBMs. The 1,300-nautical-mile SS-N-6 missile originally carried by the YANKEEs is being replaced with slightly longer-range weapons, some with multiple warheads (MRV). The SS-N-8 carried by the DELTAs has a range of over 4,000 nautical miles, while the SS-N-18 carried on the later DELTA variants provide increased range, more accuracy, and, in some models, multiple independently targetable warheads (MIRV).

In mid-1983 the relative strengths of the U.S. and Soviet fleets in numbers of modern ballistic missile submarines and submarine launched missiles were:

Soviet sailors regularly exercise in chemical-biological-radiological protective gear and their ships are especially designed to fight in the CBR environment. U.S. Navy capabilities in these areas are severely limited, especially with regard to protective measures.

Figure 1
BALLISTIC MISSILE SUBMARINES AND MISSILES

	United States	Soviet Union
Modern Submarines (Nuclear)*	34	62
Older Submarines (Nuclear)	0	2
Older Submarines (Diesel)	0	15
SLBMs in modern submarines	568	920
SLBMs in older submarines	—	58

The Soviets have been adhering to the total of 62 modern missile submarines allowed under the terms of SALT I by removing the missile tubes from the older YANKEEs. The U.S. has decommissioned or modified the ten oldest (Polaris) SSBNs to compensate for the commissioning of the OHIO-class SSBNs.

Today, U.S. submarines and strategic missiles are believed to be qualitatively superior to the Soviet weapons in several key categories; however, that qualitative advantage is being narrowed as Soviet development efforts continue at a rapid pace.

Admiral Gorshkov emphasized the development of antiship missiles. By the late 1950s several missiles were at sea, including the SS-N-2 STYX. At top, Soviet sailors lower a STYX into a launch tube and, above, an OSA missile boat fires a STYX.

When the lead TRIDENT submarine, the USS OHIO, was delivered in 1981, the U.S. Navy took delivery of its first new strategic missile submarine since 1967. Since that date the Soviets have completed 70 modern SSBNs with construction continuing. In addition, several older GOLF II (diesel) and HOTEL (nuclear) submarines are estimated to still be operational with ballistic missiles. Although these submarines have missiles with a range of only about 700 nautical miles, they do pose a threat in the European theater and western Pacific.

The large commitment of resources that the Soviet leaders have allocated to their sea-based nuclear strike force is indicative of the vital importance of that force.

Maritime Security

The mission of providing for the maritime security of the Soviet Union includes both strategic and tactical defense tasks to eliminate naval threats against the Soviet homeland. This is an expansion of the Navy's tradition "defense of the homeland" mission. Soviet naval forces are very aggressively and offensively oriented in exercising these "defensive" tasks; the Soviets are firm believers in the old adage, "the best defense is a good offense."

Included in the mission of maritime security is the destruction of enemy naval forces, particularly those that pose a strategic threat to the Soviet Union, such as Western strategic missile submarines and aircraft carriers. The Soviets have considerable forces available to locate and attack surface formations such as carrier and amphibious task forces. Although they have expended considerable resources in recent years on antisubmarine warfare, including an intensive ASW research and development program, it is apparent that the Soviets have not resolved the problem of locating submarines on the high seas with a high degree of probability. This task becomes progressively more difficult as longer-range missiles become available to permit submarines to operate in much larger ocean areas and still remain within range of their targets. But the Soviet ASW efforts are considerable and continuing.

Another aspect of maritime security is Soviet countering of the considerable ASW forces of the U.S. Navy and our Allies. The Soviets are thus concerned with the protection of their own SSBNs and have developed forces to attack Western ASW forces in a "defense in depth" concept. Admiral Gorshkov describes this task by noting:

Diverse warfare ships and aircraft are included in the inventory of our Navy in order to give combat stability to the submarines and comprehensively support them, to battle the enemy's surface and ASW forces. . .

In support of this mission, the Soviet Navy has developed several classes of large ASW ships which, along with specialized aircraft and submarines, appear to be intended to support Soviet submarines—a primary arm of the Soviet Navy. This is a highly specialized form of "sea control." Some of the newer classes of large ASW ships, especially the KRESTA II and KARA cruiser classes are multipurpose ships, with significant antiair warfare (AAW) and antisurface warfare (ASUW) capabilities, while the UDALOY destroyer class, with the lead ship completed in 1981, is a highly specialized antisubmarine ship.

Again, operating in conjunction with submarines (diesel as well as nuclear) and aircraft, including ship-based helicopters, these large ASW ships can permit the Soviets to exercise their own type of sea control to provide maritime security for their own submarines as well as surface strike forces, amphibious and merchant convoys, and replenishment ships.

Sea-Line Interdiction

The interdiction of Western sea lines of communication (SLOC) has been a mission of the Soviet Navy since the beginning of the "cold war". The relative importance of SLOC interdiction within the hierarchy of Soviet naval missions has fluctuated, depending on the current perceptions of the likely nature and length of a NATO-Warsaw Pact conflict. If such a war were nuclear and of short duration, Soviet anti-SLOC operations would be of little consequence. But since the advancement of NATO's "flexible response" strategy, as well as increased conventional and nuclear capabilities on the Soviet side, the Soviets have written more frequently about the possibilities of a conventional war and prolonged conflict.

Although the extent and timing of a SLOC interdiction campaign would depend on the nature of the initial stage of the conflict, the Soviets have clearly indicated that they regard SLOC interdiction as an important task. They have a large capability in their submarine and air forces to fight such a campaign once the decision to do so has been made. As Admiral Gorshkov has recently said:

. . . the disruption of the ocean line of communications, the special arteries feeding the

Soviet Naval Infantry practice beach assault disembarking from their amphibious BTR-60 armored personnel carriers.

military and economic potentials of those (the enemy) countries, has continued to be one of the most important of the Navy's missions.

Support Of Ground Forces

The Soviet Union's geographical position and its consequent status as primarily a land power demand that the Soviet Navy protect the seaward flanks of the army. Although the Soviet Navy has been recast into an ocean-going force with major offensive as well as defensive tasks, support of the ground forces still remains an important mission. This task, of course, entails protecting the army's seaward flanks from attack by enemy naval and amphibious forces, providing naval gunfire and logistics support and carrying out amphibious assaults in support of land operations. The operations involved would appear to be most likely in the Baltic and Black Seas as spearheads to obtain control of the Danish and Turkish Straits, respectively, and also in assaults against Northern Norway and possibly the Japanese Straits.

The Soviets maintain several SVERDLOV class cruisers, with 12 six-inch guns, and a large short-range assault force of amphibious ships and naval infantry ("marines"), presumably to conduct flanking operations and to seize key coastal areas in support of ground operations. Soviet military doctrine calls for the small naval infantry force, to make initial landings, to be followed by army units that are specially trained in amphibious operations. Several army divisions periodically practice amphibious landings, and a large and readily adaptable merchant fleet is available to supplement the amphibious ships in supporting these movements. Airborne operations are often conducted in conjunction with amphibious exercises. Also, the diesel and nuclear powered submarines armed with short range ballistic missiles apparently have theater strike roles in support of ground operations. In 1976 six GOLF II class SSBs, each with three 700-nautical-mile nuclear ballistic missiles, were the first submarines to be assigned to the Baltic Fleet in this role.

Support of State Policy

The Soviet leadership in the last two decades has awakened to the value of a powerful navy and other

11

elements of sea power as tangible support for their nation's foreign economic, political and military policies. The Soviets have discovered the tenets which Alfred Thayer Mahan postulated in his book *The Influence of Sea Power Upon History* (1890), and what some of the tsars before them realized: a navy is well suited for an active and useful role as an instrument of state policy in peacetime as well as in wartime.

Because of its great operational flexibility, its visibility and the lack of political restraints on the movement of warships on the high seas, a fleet is able to demonstrate power in distant areas to support national objectives. Of all the armed services, a navy is best suited for this world-wide role because it is not restricted by the sovereignty of airspace over land or by territorial rights.

The tutor to the Kremlin in naval matters, Admiral Gorshkov, has stated:

Warships appearing directly off the shore represent a real threat of operations whose time and execution are determined by those in command. Whereas such a threat was quite great in the past, today it is much more so, since modern warships are platforms for nuclear-missile weaponry and aircraft whose range can cover the entire territory of a state.

The Soviet Navy maintains a fleet in the Mediterranean on a continuous basis. Seen here at the southern entrance to the Aegean Sea are, clockwise from top, a KASHIN missile destroyer, a VYTEGRALES class cargo ship, a KASHIN with a NANUCHKA missile ship astern, and a KOTLIN destroyer with a NANUCHKA astern.

He has also written:

Navies . . . are constantly being utilized as an instrument of state policy in peacetime. In this regard, navies have assumed particular significance under today's conditions. The mobility of the fleet and its flexibility in the event limited military conflicts are brewing, permit it to have an influence on coastal countries, to employ and extend a military threat to any level, beginning with a show of military strength and ending with the landing of forces ashore.

Taking Admiral Gorshkov at his word, one can observe that "support of state policy" goes beyond the peacetime "showing the flag" role. In recent years the Soviets have not been timid in using their Navy to support client states and friends in time of crisis. Prime examples have been the regular Soviet naval and air operations in the Caribbean in support of Communist Cuba, during the Indo-Pakistani conflict of 1971, in the Middle East during the 1973 Arab-Israeli conflict, the 1975 intervention of the USSR and Cuba in the Angolian civil war, the Ethiopian civil war of 1978, and the Sino-Vietnam conflict of the same year.

Today, Soviet naval forces are deployed continuously on several seas and perform a variety of political and military tasks. They demonstrate Soviet military might during port visits, assert Soviet rights on the high seas, protect the interests of Soviet merchant and fishing fleets, demonstrate support for Soviet clients and inhibit Western military initiatives: The Russian bear has grown webbed feet.

E. The Future

The Soviet Navy can be expected to seek to expand its capabilities in various functional areas in the years to come. The Soviets might seek to expand their now limited ability to extend conventional power ashore to areas distant from the Soviet Union into a full-fledged seaborne projection capability with its attendant sea control, amphibious assault and sea-based aviation forces. This possibility is discussed further in Section 4.

As the Soviet Union expands its world trade and becomes increasingly dependent on foreign commodities and imported technology, it will find it necessary to provide protection to its distant sea lines of communications.

Another emerging mission for the Soviet Navy, as well as the other navies of the world, will be the protection of facilities exploiting ocean economic resources. With or without the introduction of a new International Law of the Sea Treaty, exploitation of the seabed and fishing resources will become an increasingly important issue among the world's nations.

Section 3. The Soviet Navy Today

Our country has built a modern Navy and sent it out into the ocean in order to support our own state interests and to reliably defend us from attack from the vast ocean sector.

Admiral of the Fleet of the Soviet Union
S.G. GORSHKOV

The Soviet Navy has dramatically increased at sea operations since the early 1960s with particular emphasis in political-economic crisis areas such as the eastern Mediterranean and Indian Ocean. Along with this quantitative increase there has been an increase in warship capabilities. At the same time, U.S. naval forces and operations have declined considerably.

A. Operations

Today the Soviet Navy maintains ships at sea in a number of areas of the world far distant from the U.S.S.R. Descriptions of these ships, their weapons and their crews are found in subsequent sections of this publication.

Long range deployments have increased dramatically since the early 1960s. Until then, Soviet ships remained primarily in coastal areas, adjacent to their major fleet operating bases in the Baltic Sea, Arctic Ocean and Northwest Pacific Ocean. After Admiral Gorshkov's "go to sea" order of 1963, a dramatic increase in Soviet operations outside of coastal areas began. Figure 2 shows this trend, with U.S. Navy ship deployments provided for comparison. U.S. operations decreased dramatically in the early 1970s, partially as a result of the reduction of our active fleet by almost one-half of its peak strength during the Vietnam War (1967–1968).

Submarines

From the 1960s onward there has been a marked increase in submarine activity involving torpedo and cruise missile attack submarines and strategic missile submarines. The latter has particular significance because of the greatly reduced flight time of 8 to 12 minutes of the SS-N-6 SLBM compared to the 20 to 30-minute flight time of intercontinental ballistic missiles (ICBMs) launched from the Soviet Union, or the several-hour flight time of manned bombers from the Soviet Union to attack targets in the United States. The Soviet SLBM capability could threaten U.S. bomber bases as well as national command centers, possibly destroying bombers and "pinning down" missiles before they could be launched. (SLBMs currently are considered to lack the accuracy to destroy Minuteman ICBMs in hardened underground silos.)

The earliest Soviet strategic-missile submarines, constructed in the late 1950s, posed little threat to the continental United States. These submarines had limited underwater endurance, could only fire missiles while on the surface, and were armed with only two or three SARK (SS-N-4) missiles which had a range of about 350 nautical miles and poor accuracy. (Many of these earlier SSBs and SSBNs were later equipped with 700 NM range SS-N-5 missiles). These submarines apparently had major problems. One GOLF class was lost in the North Pacific in 1968 and one HOTEL class SSBN experienced serious engine trouble in the North Atlantic early in 1972. (The HOTEL was towed back to the Soviet Union on the surface.)

The Soviet SLBM situation changed radically in 1967 when they sent their first YANKEE class submarine to sea. This nuclear powered submarine, armed with 16 SS-N-6 missiles having an initial range of 1,300 nautical miles and capable of submerged launch, was more difficult to detect and had a potent strike capability. During 1968, YANKEE class SSBNs began patrols in the Atlantic, periodically coming within range of U.S. cities. In 1971, YANKEE SSBN patrols began off the Pacific coast. The later DELTA class SSBNs, with a missile range in excess of 4,000 nautical miles, are within

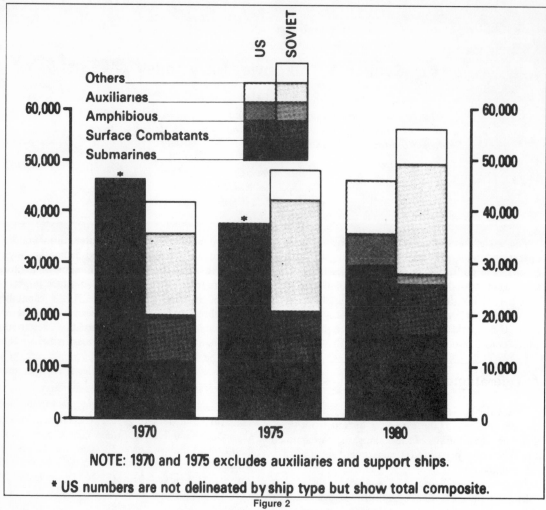

NOTE: 1970 and 1975 excludes auxiliaries and support ships.

* US numbers are not delineated by ship type but show total composite.

Figure 2
Trends in U.S.-Soviet Out-of-Area Ship Days

striking distance of New York City or Washington, D.C. while still in well protected Soviet home port areas on the Arctic coast. This same situation applies in the Pacific, where DELTA class SSBNs at their base of Petropavlovsk on the Siberian coast are within missile range of western U.S. cities such as Seattle and San Francisco.

A related development in Soviet SSBN development has been construction of the TYPHOON-class submarines, the first of which was completed in 1983. The TYPHOON is the world's largest undersea craft, with a submerged displacement estimated at some 25,000 tons. Carrying 20 large, long-range SS-N-20 ballistic missiles, the TYPHOON appears to have been designed specifically to operate under the Arctic ice pack. A missile submarine under the ice is relatively difficult

for U.S. antisubmarine forces to detect and attack.

Whereas less than two decades ago the Soviets had a relatively small force of strategic submarines with a few short-range missiles, today's Soviet missile submarines provide a significant and increasing percentage of Soviet strategic nuclear strike capability.

The massive Soviet SSBN effort, which has produced more than 70 nuclear-powered submarines in 15 years, has not detracted from Soviet attack submarine programs. Several classes of nuclear and diesel submarines armed with torpedoes and cruise missiles have also been produced in large numbers. These general-purpose submarines now roam the world's oceans in support of Kremlin policies, ready to challenge an adversary's use of the sea.

The modernization of the Soviet submarine force

has resulted in an approximately level force during the past decade with improvements in ship performance, weapons, and sensors. When this edition went to press the Soviets had seven nuclear and two diesel attack submarine classes under construction with about eight attack submarines (SS/SSN/SSGN) per year being completed. (In addition, FOXTROT-class diesel submarines are still being produced for foreign users.)

Mediterranean

The most significant Soviet deployments have been in the crisis-plagued Eastern Mediterranean. Soviet out-of-area ship days in the Mediterranean increased from approximately 4,000 in 1965 to more than 16,500 in 1979. An out-of-area ship day is defined as one in which a navy ship is deployed beyond the normal operating and training areas of home waters. Thus, 16,500 ship days means an average of about 45 ships in the area every day of the year. In the early 1970s the Soviets apparently achieved the general levels of deployments they perceived as adequate for "support of state interest" purposes. Usually, 10 to 15 percent of the Soviet ocean going fleet is operating "out-of-area." The Kremlin leadership, however, has been quick to increase the number of deployed ships to areas of crisis or elsewhere for other perceived needs.

The Soviet Mediterranean fleet normally consists of:

6 to	8	torpedo attack submarines
1 or	2	cruise missile attack submarines
1 or	2	cruisers, and periodically aviation ships of the MOSKVA and KIEV classes
6 to	8	destroyers and frigates
1 to	3	minesweepers
1 to	3	amphibious ships
15 to	20	auxiliary ships
5 or	6	survey, oceanographic research, and intelligence collection ships

The presence of these ships increases Soviet political and military options in the Mediterranean. For example, shortly after the June 1967 Arab-Israeli war began, the Soviets sent ships to the Egyptian harbors of Port Said and Alexandria in an obvious move to deter Israeli attacks against those ports.

The air bases in Egypt, used by the Soviets from 1967 until 1972, permitted Soviet land-based naval reconnaissance and ASW aircraft to operate over the eastern Mediterranean without overflying Greece or Turkey. The loss of Egyptian air bases to the Soviets in 1972 unquestionably reduced Soviet military capabilities in the eastern Mediterranean. However, the Soviet naval position in 1972 after loss of the air bases was still far superior to that of a decade earlier.

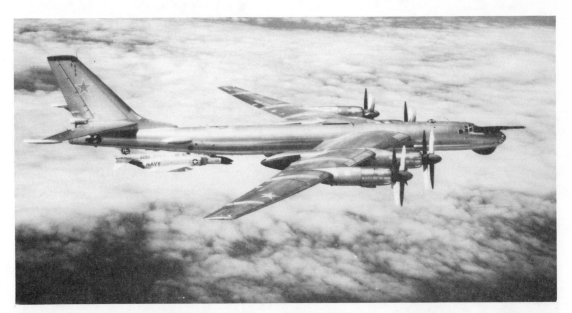

The large BEAR D aircraft provides the Soviet Navy with long-range reconnaissance and missile targeting. Note the counter-rotating propellers on the BEAR's four turboprop engines, the "chin" radome (there is a larger "belly" radome), and the nose refueling probe. A U.S. Navy F-4 Phantom flies "escort" as this BEAR nears a U.S. carrier.

In addition to the large number of fighter aircraft provided by the Soviets to Middle Eastern countries, BLINDER supersonic bombers have also been delivered to Iraq and Libya.

A large number of missile-armed patrol boats have been delivered by the Soviets to Third World countries in the Mediterranean, as well as diesel torpedo-attack submarines of the FOXTROT class to Libya and WHISKEY and ROMEO classes to Egypt.

The Soviets continue to press for base facilities on the Mediterranean littoral. Besides limited base support facilities in use in Tartus, Syria, the Soviet Navy, on a contract basis, utilizes overhaul and repair facilities at shipyards in Yugoslavia, Tunisia and Greece. The naval leadership no doubt desires more permanent arrangements for bases with greater facilities than presently available to them. A prime candidate from the Soviet point of view must be the old French naval base of Mers-el-Kabir in Algeria.

The Soviet Mediterranean Squadron (SOVMEDRON) is maintained and supplied primarily at anchorages in international waters. Although this routine is adequate in peacetime, under wartime conditions such a logistics operation would be most vulnerable.

Although their Navy operates in the Mediterranean under a number of restrictive conditions, the Soviets are constantly striving to eliminate or minimize those restrictions. Access to the gates of the Mediterranean is controlled by powers outside the Soviet sphere of influence: the Suez Canal is con-

The nuclear guided missile cruiser KIROV—often referred to as a "battlecruiser"—carries a large, multi-purpose armament. She has a combination nuclear-oil burning steam plant, providing long range and high speed.

trolled by Egypt; the Atlantic egress by Spain and the British bastion at Gibraltar; and the Turkish Straits to the Black Sea by Turkey, a member of NATO. The Turkish Straits are also regulated by an international treaty, the Montreux Convention, which the Soviets probably perceive more as a blessing than a curse. Although Soviet warships must give advance notice and are restricted in the numbers which may pass through per day, navies of countries not washed by Black Sea waters have much greater restrictions placed upon their warships operating in that sea.

From all appearances the Soviets look upon the eastern Mediterranean as *"Mare Nostrum,"* and consider those waters critical to their national defense. Because of this they will no doubt continue to strive for port access and base facilities as well as overflight rights as they work to extend their political influence in the Mediterranean area. They will undoubtedly continue in their attempts to weaken NATO's southern flank by driving a wedge between the West and the vital Mid-east by flexing naval muscle in this historic cross roads of civilizations and cultures—the Mediterranean Sea.

Caribbean

Soviet naval deployments to the Caribbean began in mid-1969 when a task force consisting of a missile-armed cruiser, two missile-armed destroyers, three attack submarines (one nuclear powered) and three auxiliary ships operated in the Caribbean, making port visits to Cuba.

One year later, another Soviet task force operated in the Caribbean and still others have subsequently steamed in those waters. On past occasions, nuclear powered cruise missile submarines and conventionally powered GOLF class ballistic missile submarines have operated in Cuban waters. On a number of occasions these ships have operated in the Gulf of Mexico off the Louisiana and Texas coasts. Besides showing the flag in the Caribbean, these Soviet warships have participated often in training exercises with Cuban naval units. Through 1979, there had been 20 naval deployments to Cuba, in addition to the stationing of a fleet tug there and regular replenishment visits by intelligence collectors and survey ships. In this regard, the Soviets have shown a varying interest in the naval base at Cienfuegos on the south coast of Cuba. The Cuban Navy is now provided almost entirely with Soviet equipment, including two FOXTROT class submarines.

In April of 1970, a pair of long-range BEAR D naval reconnaissance aircraft flew non-stop from bases in the Murmansk area on the soviet Arctic coast, down the Norwegian Sea, across the Atlantic, and landed in Cuba. Other naval BEAR reconnaissance and ASW aircraft have followed in what has developed into a continuous schedule, with some aircraft flying reconnaissance missions off the U.S. Atlantic coast during these flights. (One of these aircraft was accidently lost off Newfoundland in November 1975.) Because the Soviets can no longer use airfields in Guinea, West Africa, BEAR deployments to and from Angola now stage through Cuba, usually in pairs.

The periodic presence of Soviet naval ships in the Caribbean, along with a brigade of troops in Cuba, demonstrates Soviet support for the Castro government. This presence could inhibit U.S. politico-military options in the area inasmuch as their presence implies support for intervention or revolution in the Central American region.

The periodic presence of U.S.S.R. naval ships in the Caribbean demonstrates Soviet support for the Castro government. This presence could inhibit U.S. options in the area inasmuch as their presence inplies support for intervention or revolution in Central American nations.

Atlantic

Over the past two decades the Soviet Navy has regularly exercised in the Norwegian Sea. Their major efforts are concentrated in the spring in contrast to annual NATO naval exercises, usually held in the fall. Most Soviet exercise activity has taken place north of the Greenland-Iceland-United Kingdom (GIUK) gap. In recent years, however, Soviet submarines, surface warships, and aircraft have operated more frequently further south in the Western Approaches to Europe. This is in addition to those units transiting the area for the Mediterranean or Cuba or to the open ocean for ballistic missile patrols.

Besides the aforementioned activity, the Soviets regularly maintain intelligence collection ships (AGI) on patrol off the Western SSBN bases in Scotland, the United States and until its disestablishment in 1979, the base at Rota, Spain.

In the South Atlantic, Soviet warships have maintained a nearly continuous patrol off the African west coast since late 1970. The appearance of these ships in the Gulf of Guinea "coincided" with the release by the Accra government of two Soviet fishing craft impounded some months earlier. Further, Soviet warships appeared in the aftermath of a Portugese-supported raid against Conakry, Guinea in November 1970, possible in an effort to deter further attacks.

19

Starting in the Spring of 1973, pairs of naval BEAR D reconnaissance aircraft made periodic deployments to Conakry, Guinea, from the Soviet Arctic to fly surveillance missions against U.S. Navy ships in the Central Atlantic.

During the Angolan civil war in 1975–1976, Soviet warships were dispatched to patrol the waters near Angola as an encouragement for the Soviet backed Cuban intervention in support of one of the rebel groups. Simultaneously, Soviet aircraft flew in Cuban troops and supplies while the Soviet merchant marines mounted a massive sealift of war material. Since that time, BEAR D reconnaissance aircraft have occasionally operated out of Luanda, Angola, which allows this aircraft coverage of most of the South Atlantic.

Aside from the small South African Navy, the Soviet West African squadron is the only continuous naval presence in that area of the South Atlantic, astride the vital oil route from the Persian Gulf to Western Europe.

Indian Ocean

Soviet ships regularly operate in the Indian Ocean, generally with a missile-armed cruiser, several destroyers, an amphibious ship, a submarine and a number of support ships. (The Soviet squadron averaged about 20 ships until the crisis of 1979-80 when the average was about 30.) These ships demonstrate support of Soviet interests on the coasts of the three continents washed by the Indian Ocean. This regular deployment, which commenced in 1968, has been the key element in Soviet relations with India and several of the newer countries in the area.

The Soviets' need for port access and base facilities in the Indian Ocean is even greater than that in the Mediterranean Sea. A glance at a globe will show the great transit distance from Soviet Pacific and Black Sea bases (particularly if the Suez Canal is closed) to the Indian Ocean. A look at the southern border of the U.S.S.R. in the Trans-Caucasus area reveals what drives the historical Russian desire to gain direct access to the Indian Ocean, which no doubt contributed to the Soviet decision to invade Afghanistan in late 1979.

During the 1970s, the Soviets built several naval and air facilities in Somalia in a strategic position to control the Red Sea and access to the Suez Canal. In 1977, after a falling-out with the regime in Somalia, the Soviets were forced out of their bases there. They subsequently resorted to the use of facilities in Aden, South Yemen, and Ethiopia, to support their Indian Ocean Squadron (SOVINDRON). MAY maritime patrol aircraft, operating from Aden, have frequently tracked U.S. naval units in the Arabian Sea. During the recent buildup of forces as a result of the Iran and Afghan crises, the Soviets operated as many as six MAYs from Aden and Ethiopia.

The Soviet Indian Ocean squadron also has used port facilities in Iraq in the past, and regularly makes calls to selected ports on the Indian Ocean littoral. Soviet naval ships visit ports in Mozambique, the Seychelles Islands, Mauritius, India, and Sri Lanka.

The Soviets have shown a willingness to expand their naval commitment in the Indian Ocean whenever they believe their interests to be threatened. During the Indian-Pakistan War of 1971; immediately after the Arab-Israeli War of 1973; in support of Ethiopian-Somalia conflict; during the Iranian revolution in early 1979 and the Iranian hostage crisis; and the Afghanistan invasion in late 1979, the Soviets increased the number of warships deployed to the Indian Ocean including cruise missile submarines. This served to counter U.S. carrier forces, which had been sent from the Pacific and Atlantic Fleets as well as to support their "clients."

In the aftermath of the Arab-Israeli and Indian-Pakistan wars the Soviet Navy provided harbor clearance and minesweeping services to both Bangledesh and Egypt, respectively. They helped in clearing the port of Chittagong and the southern approaches to the Suez Canal. One of the ships involved in the Suez operation was the aviation cruiser LENINGRAD.

Although the Suez Canal is now open, making the area "east of Suez" more accessible to the Soviet Black Sea Fleet, the majority of Soviet ships which deploy to the Indian Ocean make the long trip from the Pacific Ocean Fleet. It is on long transits such as these that the Soviets often tow submarines and smaller combatants as one way of reducing "wear and tear" on these ships, extending the time between engine overhauls and conserving fuel.

With the termination of extensive Bangledesh and Egyptian operations in 1974 the number of Soviet naval ships and, therefore, the total number of "ship days" in the Indian Ocean dropped to "normal" numbers. The Soviets now average a force of about 20 ships in the Indian Ocean, the majority of which are naval auxiliaries. In comparison, the U.S. Navy's standing commitment to the Indian Ocean area consists of one amphibious ship converted to a flagship and two or three destroyers or frigates.

U.S. carrier task forces have deployed periodically to the Indian Ocean, but only with considerable difficulty in ship scheduling and logistics. Since late

1979, with the Iran crisis and the invasion of Afghanistan by the Soviets, both the U.S. and Soviet naval commitments in the Indian Ocean have, nonetheless, expanded significantly.

Pacific Ocean

In the Pacific, the Soviets initiated long range surface ship operations during the 1950s when relations between Moscow and Peking were amiable. Subsequently, aid to Indonesia and other Soviet interests in the Pacific basin led to expanded Soviet naval operations.

During the fall of 1971 a Soviet force consisting of a guided-missile cruiser, two missile-armed destroyers, three submarines and a tanker crossed the Pacific to the Gulf of Alaska, and then turned south to steam within 25 miles of Diamond Head, Hawaii, before returning to Soviet Pacific coast ports. Soviet Pacific Ocean Fleet ships were used to collect intelligence and as an occasional show of force against U.S. Seventh Fleet during the Vietnam War. Soviet warships periodically visit many parts of the Pacific where, until a decade ago, Soviet military power was discussed but never seen. As an example, two Soviet missile destroyers and an oiler made a port visit to Vancouver, Canada in 1976.

Soviet AGIs are regularly deployed off Guam to monitor the arrivals and departures of U.S. ballistic missile submarines operating from there. AGIs also operate off the U.S. West Coast with some regularity. A number of Soviet space support and recovery ships deploy to the North Central Pacific, an area into which the Soviets test fire their long-range ballistic missiles.

Recently the Soviet Navy has been using port facilities and airfields in Vietnam to support expanded deployments in the South China Sea. Soviet naval presence increased in this area during the Sino-Vietnam War of 1979. This increased presence has been maintained and includes the regular deployment of BEAR D and F aircraft.

B. Trends

An analysis of the Soviet Navy during the past two decades reveals (1) significant diversity and improvement in warship, aircraft, and weapons capabilities; (2) large increases in at-sea and distant deployment operations; (3) commitments by the Soviets to strive for a Navy "second to none;" and (4) increased awareness by the Soviet leadership of the leverage which accures to a nation with sizeable and strong maritime resources, especially a large, modern navy.

Several comparisons of trends related to the U.S. and Soviet navies support these observations.

The Soviet Navy is by far the largest in the world today in terms of numbers of ships, primarily be-

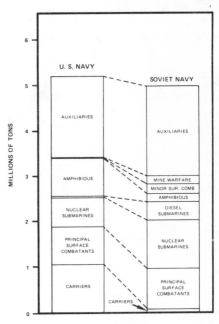

FIGURE 3
NUMBER OF ACTIVE SHIPS 1979

FIGURE 4
FULL LOAD DISPLACEMENT OF SHIPS IN COMMISSION 1979

cause of the large numbers of submarines, small combatants, mine warfare ships, and auxiliaries in its inventory. While the preceding is an important point, estimating the relative capabilities of navies is not just a matter of comparing force levels, or matching distant deployments and exercises. All of these are factors in estimating the naval balance, but just as important are weapons, sensors, communications, and personnel, as well as trends in doctrine, development, procurement, and national will and commitment. In assessing the relative merits of navies, the prime point is which navy can best accomplish its mission under the real or potential threat of its adversaries.

Although the total numerical inventory is slowly declining, for the foreseeable future the Soviet Navy is expected to continue to have the world's largest number of warships.

It cannot be ignored that as a result of the Soviet leadership's determined policy to expand all facets of the sea power equation, the Soviet Navy is continuing to expand its recently acquired "blue water" capabilities. Indications are those efforts will not diminish over the next few years.

Figures 3 and 4 depict the comparisons of the numbers and tonnages between the various ship categories in the Soviet Navy and the U.S. Navy. It should be noted that the U.S. Navy greatly exceeds the Soviet Fleet in aircraft carriers; and although the Soviet Navy has more amphibious ships, the U.S. Navy amphibious lift capability is much greater. Figure 4 demonstrates that if one subtracts the U.S. Navy's 13 aircraft carriers, the Soviet Navy has a greater tonnage. Thus, the U.S. Navy's tonnage ad-

vantage and most capable conventional strike capabilities are in a fewer number of ships. However, the Soviets have numerical and tonnage leadership in several important categories.

Surface Combatants

The number of Soviet principal surface combatants (frigates and larger) is greater than that of the U.S. Navy, although more than 100 of the Soviet ships are frigates which are significantly smaller than their U.S. counterparts.

The principal surface combatants which the Soviets are building today have greater range, firepower, and electronics capabilities than in the past. The modern ships of the Soviet Navy are among the fastest and most heavily armed in the world. They are of innovative modern design, graceful yet purposeful in appearance, and have contributed greatly to elevating the prestige and power of the Soviet Union among the world's nations.

Present building programs include series production of four large surface warships: The 28,000-ton KIROV-class nuclear battle cruisers, the KRASINA-class antisurface cruisers, the SOVREMENNYY-class antisurface destroyers, and the UDALOY-class ASW destroyer.

The Soviet Navy has led the world in the use of cruise-missiles in naval warfare. Since the installation of the SS-N-1 cruise missile on the KILDEN and KRUPNYY classes of destroyers in the late 1950s, the Soviets have extensively developed and deployed this type of weapon. Today the Soviet Navy has over 20 cruisers, carriers, and destroyers;

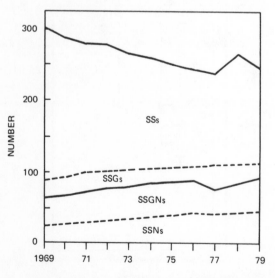

Figure 5. SOVIET GENERAL PURPOSE SUBMARINES

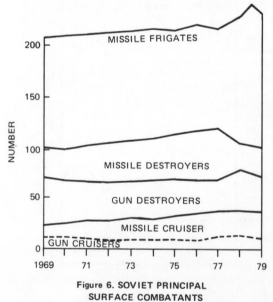

Figure 6. SOVIET PRINCIPAL
SURFACE COMBATANTS

The underway replenishment ship BORIS CHILIKIN refuels the helicopter carrier MOSKVA at sea. After long relying primarily on their merchant marine for overseas support of naval forces, the Soviets are building a large force of modern UNREP ships.

about 65 submarines; and 300 land-based aircraft armed with antiship cruise missiles. The first major U.S. weapon of this type, the HARPOON, entered service in 1977 (nearly 20 years after introduction of missiles to the Soviet Navy). The U.S. Navy had not emphasized the development of the cruise missile as an antiship weapon because of greater capabilities inherent in carrier aircraft. However, as the number of our aircraft carriers was reduced, the development of the HARPOON and TOMAHAWK cruise missiles was undertaken by the U.S. Navy. An ambitious HARPOON installation plan for aircraft, submarines and surface combatants will greatly reduce the Soviet cruise missile advantage. Although the U.S. Navy may close the gap in numbers of cruise missile systems and sophistication of guidance systems, the Soviets will, in some of their systems, retain an advantage in range and warhead size.

Critics often tend to write off the threat from the Soviet's smaller combatants (those less than 1,000 tons). For the most part they operate close to the Soviet coasts; however, the Soviets continue to pay attention to their coastal forces for obvious reasons. The Soviet Union is surrounded by a number of strong coastal navies which are viewed as threats.

This situation exists to varying degrees in all four fleet areas, but it is greatest in the Baltic. Thus, the Soviets maintain the world's largest small combatant force (many units of which are missile armed) and the largest mine warfare force as a means of controlling their coastal seas. Periodically these coastal forces operate in the regional sea such as the Norwegian and Mediterranean, where they can directly threaten U.S. naval forces.

The Soviets have developed several new types of small combatants with emphasis on hydrofoil design, missile armament and gas-turbine power.

Submarines

The soviets have led the world in the production of submarines in the post-World War II period. Since the end of the war, Soviet shipyards have built some 700 submarines (compared to less than 200 for the United States). Of particular significance has been the Soviet emphasis on nuclear-powered submarines. The Soviet Union has completed significantly more and larger nuclear-powered submarines than the United States.

The Soviet Union maintains a large submarine

construction capacity which they have expanded significantly in the past decade. Submarine production is currently being used at less than 50 percent of its estimated capacity. Submarines are produced in five building yards in the U.S.S.R., while presently only two U.S. yards are constructing submarines. The hugh shipbuilding complex at Severodvinsk on the White Sea may well have a greater nuclear submarine building capacity than that of the United States, Great Britain and France combined.

Over the last several years the Soviets have built eight or nine new submarines a year, most of them nuclear powered. U.S. submarine construction has shifted up and down dramatically; the U.S. Navy will complete one TRIDENT SSBN and about three SSNs per year during the next few years. The Soviets are expected to continue to build submarines at about the present rate.

The Soviets have built diesel and nuclear powered submarines which can launch cruise missiles. The U.S. Navy is just beginning to deploy the HARPOON missile in submarines, and is developing a submarine-launched TOMAHAWK. The Soviets have also developed a weapon similar to the U.S. Navy's SUBROC, an underwater-launched missile which flies a relatively short distance and carries an antisubmarine torpedo or nuclear depth charge.

The Soviet Navy continues to build diesel submarines to fill what Admiral Gorshkov says is a continuing need, the TANGO and KILO classes, modern attack submarines for fleet use, and the ubiquitous FOXTROT class, the latter for foreign sales. Diesel powered auxiliary submarines are also being built probably for rescue and research work.

The Soviet submarine force remains as tne dominant branch of the Soviet Navy. Although the total number of submarines has been slowly decreasing as older diesel craft are retired, the numbers of nuclear powered and missile-armed submarines continues to increase. In comparison with U.S. submarines, it is estimated the Soviets still lag in antisubmarine sensor and weapon capabilities as well as submarine quieting techniques.

Aviation

Soviet Naval Aviation has taken two significant steps in the last several years: the introduction of a sea-based, fixed-wing capability on the aircraft carrier KIEV and the introduction of the swing-wing, supersonic, missile-armed BACKFIRE bomber.

The Vertical Take-Off and Landing (VTOL) FOR-

The Soviet Navy's long-range capabilities have been enhanced by the large size of their new warships, as the carrier MINSK and KARA-class missile cruiser shown here, and modern underway replenishment ships, as the BORIS BUTOMA of the BORIS CHILIKIN class.

GER aircraft can operate from the KIEV class carriers. Although of limited capabilities, the FORGER nevertheless gives a new dimension to the Soviet Navy. It is the embryo of what the Soviets have always lacked, the ability to provide air cover and air striking power as an indigenous part of a fleet operating in distant waters.

Soviet naval leaders stopped "bad-mouthing" aircraft carriers a number of years ago and now openly advocate carriers larger than the KIEV class. There is considerable evidence that the Soviets will introduce a larger carrier class sometime in the late 1980s. It appears logical that such a large carrier would probably be nuclear powered and operate conventional takeoff and landing (CTOL) aircraft.

It is significant that supersonic BACKFIRE bombers are being supplied to the Navy in about the same numbers as they are to the Soviet Air Forces' Long Range Aviation. The antiship mission of Soviet Naval Aviation remains a high priority.

The airborne ASW components of the Soviet Navy consists of HORMONE, HAZE, and the new HELIX helicopters, and MAIL, MAY, and BEAR F fixed-wing aircraft. Over the last decade the Soviets have undertaken considerable research and development on ekronoplanes or "Wing-In-Ground" (WIG) effect vehicles. Some of this effort has been directed toward naval applications. Speculation is that the Soviets could be developing an antisubmarine or transport type WIG.

Soviet Exercises

Coupled with the increase in ship numbers and capabilities, there has been a related increase in at-sea operations, as discussed previously. As Soviet warships have gone farther from their home ports and spent more time on the high seas, they have also increased the complexity of their naval exercises. To date the largest of these were two OKEAN (Russian for ocean) exercises conducted in the spring of 1970 and again in 1975.

These were the two largest Soviet peacetime naval exercises in history, with warships simultaneously conducting maneuvers in Atlantic, Mediterranean, Indian, and Pacific Ocean areas. Over 200 submarines, surface combatants, and support ships participated in OKEAN 70, and about 120 ships in OKEAN 75. The maneuvers included antisubmarine, anticarrier, sea lines interdiction, convoy escort and amphibious landing operations. Land-based naval aircraft, as well as planes from the Soviet Air Defense Forces and Long-Range Aviation, participated in the maneuvers.

The electronics-laden island structure of the KIEV helps to demonstrate the allocation of technological resources by the Soviet Union to the development of a modern and highly capable fleet.

It appeared that these exercises were coordinated from Soviet Naval Headquarters in Moscow. From Soviet writings it is evident that a major aim of the exercises was to test the Soviet ocean surveillance system and the overall command, control, and communications (C^3) systems in world-wide scenarios. These two large exercises clearly demonstrated the scope and range of Soviet naval capabilities.

The Soviet Navy exercises routinely in antisubmarine, anticarrier, and amphibious warfare in home operating waters and when on distant deployments. For example, in the spring of 1977 the Northern and Baltic Fleets jointly conducted a large-scale exercise

25

in the Norwegian, Barents and Baltic Seas. Also, the Soviets conducted ASW exercises in the Gulf of Mexico with Cuban forces and combined missile attack and amphibious exercises in the Baltic with the East German and Polish navies.

In a report to Congress in 1983, the U.S. Navy's Director of Naval Intelligence, Rear Admiral John L. Butts, summed up the trends he expects in the future Soviet Navy:

> *The steady, year-after-year expansion of Soviet Navy capabilities shows no signs of slowing down. I think that the Soviets will probably maintain a fairly constant number of about 60 SSBNs well into the next decade, as the TYPHOON and its successor replace older classes. The overall number of general-purpose submarines will decline as obsolescent diesel submarines are retired, but the number of state-of-the-art nuclear-powered ones will increase. The number of principal surface warships will likely decline somewhat, but there will be more of the large, powerful ships.*

> * * *

> *Although the Soviet Navy's wartime tasks and approach to readiness should remain basically unchanged during the next decade, its capabilities to operate effectively in an expanding variety of circumstances over broader ocean areas will probably increase. We expect the quality of the Navy's material, maintenance, and personnel to further improve; its command and control system to become more responsive and survivable; and its ability to sustain combat operations to increase. Expansion of the Navy's support facilities and capabilities, advances in ocean surveillance systems, increasingly realistic training, and greater out-of-area operational experience all portend continuing improvement in the professionalism, maturity, and proficiency of the Soviet Navy.*

C. Limitations

As has already been noted, the Soviet Navy is not "ten feet" tall. The third edition of this book noted the Soviets were "five feet ten inches and growing," probably they should be characterized today as "six feet tall and growing." But the Soviet Navy does have significant problems because of its limitations. It must be noted that over the years the trends show the Soviets attempting to alleviate their problems

where they can by overcoming or minimizing their limitations. It is this trend that must concern the West, for as the Soviets expand their naval options and capabilities, the Western navies' options are reduced.

Rear Admiral Shapiro, during his congressional report, also noted several Soviet naval weaknesses. Included is a limited capability to conduct open ocean ASW and underway replenishment capability; inadequate sea-based tactical air forces; and geographical constraints which inhibit access to the open ocean.

The Soviets are seeking to improve their open-ocean ASW capability by a variety of methods. This includes extensive efforts in basic research and development in several detection fields, and a sizeable allocation of resources to ASW weapons procurement. Most modern Soviet surface combatants, a significant segment of the submarines force, and many of the combat aircraft of their navy are dedicated primarily to hunting Western submarines. Fortunately, their capability to find them does not appear to be improving much.

Sea-based air power is increasing significantly, with the four KIEV-class carriers each operating 12 or 13 FORGER VTOL fighter-attack aircraft as well as 14 to 17 HORMONE/HELIX helicopters. These ships will be joined by the end of the decade by a larger, nuclear-powered carrier with conventional fixed-wing aircraft. These are complemented by land-based FITTER fighter-attack aircraft in the Baltic and Pacific Fleets, as well as land-based strike, reconnaissance, ASW, and support aircraft.

The defensive limitations of Soviet strike and reconnaissance aircraft can be mitigated somewhat by overseas basing, such as has been done periodically by Soviet naval aircraft flying from Cuba, Vietnam, Guinea, Iraq, Angola, Somalia and, until 1972, Egypt. Of course, as the Soviet Navy deploys more fighter aircraft to sea, the successful defense of formations of naval strike aircraft is more likely. Lastly, the BACKFIRE bomber has supersonic dash speed, greater range, and better low-altitude performance than its predecessor, the BADGER.

The Soviet Navy has no insurmountable problems replenishing and maintaining its distant deployed fleets during peacetime in that the Soviet Navy employs tenders and oilers in anchorages in international waters as its prime means of logistic support. Many of the oilers operate under the flag of the Soviet Merchant Marine. Although the Soviets have improved their alongside underway replenishment of liquids in recent years, their ability to transfer ammunition and other solids in the same manner is still lacking.

Additionally, shore-based logistic and repair facilities are used to varying degrees in foreign ports where the Soviets have managed to gain some degree of access. Countries which provide such facilities include Syria, Cuba, Yugoslavia, Tunisia, Guinea, Angola, South Yemen, Greece, Singapore, Ethiopia and Vietnam.

During a war such port facilities might be denied or become inaccessible, and the anchorages would be vulnerable. The underway replenishment of fuels, ammunition, consumables, and repair parts would then be required to sustain warships at great distances from their home ports in prolonged periods of conflict. The Soviet Navy has been slow in developing underway replenishment capabilities and techniques; it has almost exclusively concentrated on refueling. The movement of solid stores between ships underway, and helicopter delivery techniques, have not been practiced to a great extent although the Soviets are quite adept at these movements in anchorages. During the last ten years the Soviets have introduced the BORIS CHILIKIN class of combination oiler-stores ship, and now have some six of these sophisticated underway replenishment ships in operation. Further, a number of Soviet naval and merchant oilers can provide alongside underway refueling as well as the slower astern method traditionally used by the Soviet Navy. Several smaller types of underway replenishment ships have been built for the Navy.

To meet the demands for a greater variety of fuels, ammunition, and provisions imposed by the introduction of aircraft carriers, the Soviets built a larger, multipurpose replenishment ship which carries two helicopters for vertical replenishment and is similar to the U.S. Navy's AOR design. This ship, the 40,000 ton BEREZINA, joined the fleet in 1978.

Through the centuries, Russia has been burdened with poor physical conformation of her coasts and geographic positions with respect to access to the open oceans. Today the Soviets have lessened some of these geographic limitations. For example, the scarcity of all-weather ports has been partially overcome with extensive use of icebreakers, and northern shipyards and bases have covered building ways and floating dry docks.

In the late 1950s, the significant ocean-going ships and submarines which the Soviets would use in the Atlantic were moved from the restricted waters of the Baltic to the Northern Fleet. Although the latter fleet had to contend with the rigorous Arctic climate, and had a much greater distance to travel to gain access to the North Atlantic, that access was a relatively open seaway not restricted by straits which could be easily controlled by the West. The Baltic Fleet today consists principally of a large number of smaller warships, diesel submarines, minesweepers, and amphibious ships. It is a fleet which, along with those of the East German and Polish Navies, is designed to control the Baltic and to provide support to the ground forces operating along the Baltic coasts. Under this arrangement the geographic constraint of the Danish Straits becomes less critical to the Soviets.

Similarly, the Black Sea Fleet's ability to go to sea through the NATO controlled Turkish Straits and Aegean Sea is a lesser problem because a num-

The ASW destroyer UDALOY at high speed, with the housing to her stern-fitted variable-depth sonar in the raised position. Note the side-by-side exhaust funnels for her gas turbines, and side-by-side doors to her helicopter hangars. There is a "greenhouse" control station between the hangars.

ber of that fleet's ships normally are deployed in the Mediterranean. However, resupply from the Black Sea would be a problem in time of conflict.

The Soviet Pacific Ocean Fleet has been expanded in recent years and is now second only to the Northern Fleet in capabilities. To overcome the traditional restrictions on this fleet imposed by the Japanese Straits, the Soviets have developed a large naval complex at Petropavlovsk, on the sparsely populated Kamchatka Peninsula, which provides direct access to the Pacific Ocean. It is here that the bulk of the operational submarine force is based. But this area is at the end of a long and vulnerable supply line.

Lastly, it should be noted that where geographic conformation restricts Soviet access to the open oceans, these restrictions conversely assist the Soviets in defending those waters against Western maritime threats.

Another criticism leveled at the Soviet Navy is that it is a "one-shot" fleet, optimized for strong initial striking power with relatively limited offensive weapon reloads, namely, cruise missiles. This lack of endurance reflects Admiral Gorshkov's "battle of the first salvo" philosophy. This could be considered a limitation, but at the same time it permits the Soviet Navy to be optimized for a specific war situation. However, Soviet ships have a significant reload capability in torpedoes, guns, and surface-to-air missiles that is generally comparable to U.S. ships. Lastly, several of the new classes of warships and submarines have overcome this "shortcoming" by having an increased cruise missile load of 20 or more.

D. Salesmanship

The statement has been made that the Soviets are achieving a political and psychological impact with their maritime forces far out of proportion to their size and potential. This is believed due to often exaggerated descriptions of Soviet naval power published in the West.

Not surprisingly, the same adjective-filled descriptions are trumpeted by the Soviet press and, probably of more significance, by the press of non-aligned or "third world" nations. In the same respect that "beauty is in the eye of the beholder," so is power in the eye of the beholder. In this situation the "beholder" is, to a large extent, the world that is using the seas more than ever before in history for political, resource, trade, and military purposes.

Soviet leaders—especially Admiral Gorshkov—unabashedly boast of the scope, range, influence, and power of Soviet naval forces. Admiral Gorshkov's recent book, *Sea Power of the State,* has been widely distributed throughout the world as well as in the Soviet Union. Their navy is very much in the thoughts and words of the Soviet leadership. Whereas, as noted earlier, in the late 1950s Premier Nikita Khrushchev declared the obsolescence of big-ship surface fleets and cited cruisers as being useful only to carry admirals, the current Soviet leadership obviously has a different view of naval forces.

The regular visits of Soviet Party and State leaders as well as foreign officials to warships of the Soviet Navy demonstrate their endorsement of these ships and their operations. For example, commenting on the OKEAN exercise of 1970, the Soviet Minister of Defense at the time, the late Marshal of the Soviet Union A.A. Grechko, declared that the Navy "had grown up, strengthened, and is capable of reliably defending our state interests on the wide reaches of the world's oceans." And L.I. Brezhnev, the First Secretary of the Communist Part, has observed the reaction of the United States to Soviet naval efforts. He has explained the ability of the Soviet Navy to limit Western freedom of action by pointing to American reaction in this manner:

> *The propaganda machine of the USA has launched a whole campaign concerning the Soviet Navy. Washington, you see, perceives a threat in the fact that our vessels appear in the Mediterranean, in the Indian Ocean, and in other seas. But at the same time their Sixth Fleet is constantly in the Mediterranean—at the side, as it were, of the Soviet Union, and the Seventh Fleet—off the shores of China and Indochina.*

As Soviet naval forces deploy farther on the high seas they also are visiting more foreign ports. Admiral Gorshkov stated in the early 1970s that in the previous three-year period:

> *. . . some 1,000 combatants and auxiliary ships have visited the ports of 60 countries in Europe, Asia, Africa, and Latin America. More than 100,000 of our officers and rated and non-rated men have visited the shores of foreign states.*

What a contrast to 20 years or earlier when Soviet naval visits outside the Communist sphere did not average one per year.

As an indication that such an activity continues to increase, another Soviet admiral noted that in 1975 alone, the Navy had visited 82 ports in over 50 countries, and that some 80,000 Soviet officers and sailors had strolled on foreign shores.

Soviet sailors do not fill the local museums, restaurants, and bars as do American sailors, nor do they have significant funds. But, the Red sailors do go ashore, and their warships, modern and well kept, do ride at anchor in an increasing number of harbors. Their ships often carry bands and dance teams on these visits, and the local officials, and sometimes the public, are invited to tour the ships.

With this widespread, visible presence of the Soviet Navy in many areas of the world, and its threat of interposition as a shield to a client state or revolutionary movement (such as happened during the Angolan civil war and the Ethiopian-Somalia War), Western nations have had their peacetime political options greatly reduced. As French writer Michel Tatu observed:

> *Landings of the type carried out by the United States in Lebanon in 1958 and in the Dominican Republic in 1965 would be more hazardous, if not entirely out of the question, today. On the other hand, a landing by Soviet "marines" to support some "progressive" regime or to help some minority faction in a power struggle is no longer inconceivable.*

As a means to achieve better understanding between the two superpower navies and their personnel, the U.S. Navy and Soviet Navy exchanged port visits in 1975. The United States sent a cruiser and destroyer to Leningrad and the Soviets sent two destroyers to Boston. Both visits were generously welcomed by their respective hosts, and large, enthusiastic crowds toured the visiting ships in both countries. Also, during the 1976 Operation Sail and International Naval Review of the United States' Bicentennial Independence Day Celebration, the largest sailing ship present was the beautiful square-rigged KRUZENSHTERN, a Soviet merchant marine

The Soviet merchant marine training bark KRUZENSHTERN was the largest participating ship in Operational Sail, a gathering of tall sailing ships during the American Bicentennial Celebration. The Soviet merchant marine and fisheries industries use several sailing ships as well as more modern ships dedicated to personnel training.

training ship. Over the last several years naval protocol visits also have been exchanged between the Soviets and Britain, Canada, Sweden and France, as well as a number of other nations.

Thus, the Soviets are impressively visible, especially to those who need to use the sea for political, economic, and military purposes. The perceptions of Soviet naval and maritime prestige held by other nations have become a major factor in international relations.

In summary, Americans must keep a perspective when discussing the development, capabilities, and intentions of the Soviet Navy. We must be cautious of overstating, but, even more important, we must guard against understating the threat posed by the Soviet Navy both as a peacetime organization and a fighting force.

The Soviet Navy's first full-fledged aircraft carrier was the KIEV. Here her sistership MINSK is about to land a FORGER approaching over the fantail—note the spray being generated by the VTOL fighters' vertical lift engine.

Section 4. Soviet Naval Hardware

In the course of building our Navy, a great deal of attention was devoted and continues to be devoted to constantly maintaining all the elements comprising its combat strength in the most favorable combination, that is, as we have come to say today, to keep them balanced.

Admiral of the Fleet of the Soviet Union
S.G. GORSHKOV

The Soviet government has made a tremendous investment in ships, aircraft, weapons, sensors, and related naval hardware during the past two decades. This investment has been directed toward producing a large ocean-going fleet that is, in many respects, innovative and highly capable. However, the missions of the Soviet Navy are somewhat different from those of Western navies, as are certain personnel traits, approaches to research, industrial base, and strategy, tactics and doctrine. Hence, Soviet naval hardware is, in many respects, different from "equivalent" U.S. naval systems.

A. Surface Warships

The Soviet Navy maintains by far the world's largest fleet of principal surface combatants, patrol and coastal combatant forces. Admiral Gorshkov has stated that his surface ships are to provide "combat stability" for his prime war fighting forces, the submarines and naval aviation. The Soviets not only view their surface warships as necessary elements of a "balanced fleet," but also use their ocean-going warships as primary instruments for "showing the flag" throughout the world, providing a visible naval presence when necessary in support of Soviet foreign policy. Emphasis continues on multi-purpose, long-endurance ships more heavily armed with antisubmarine, antiair, and antiship weapons than most comparable ships in other navies.

Photographs and specifications of the surface warships are provided in Appendix C of this publication.

Aviation Ships

The widely publicized KIEV class aircraft carriers are the largest warships ever completed by the Soviet Union.* After years of criticizing U.S. carriers as being obsolete and vulnerable, Soviet naval writers began to change their professed views in the late 1960s. Grudging praise of the flexibility and mobile power represented by the modern aircraft carriers, particularly those with nuclear power, began to creep into Soviet writings and has increased in recent years.

Since 1975 the Soviets have had a sea-based, fixed-wing aircraft in service. Four of these KIEV-class VTOL aircraft carriers have been built. In addition to their 30 fixed-wing aircraft and helicopters, these ships have significant antiship, antiair, and antisubmarine weapon batteries.

The Soviets now appear to be constructing a larger aircraft carrier of some 60,000 tons, with indications that she will be nuclear propelled. This ship is expected to be completed in the late 1980s and carry *conventional take-off-and-landing* (CTOL) aircraft. The ship will have catapults and arresting gear, and can be expected to have an air wing of about 60 aircraft.

The Soviets originally classified the KIEV as a "large antisubmarine warfare cruiser," possibly because (1) that is her basic mission, (2) it was not politically acceptable to call any Soviet ship an aircraft carrier after years of deprecating remarks concerning Western carriers by Soviet military writers, (3) the Soviets may have wished to project this ship as another evolutionary development of their ASW cruiser program and not a copy of the Western aircraft carrier concept, or (4) the Soviets wished to circumvent some interpretations of the Montreux Convention which proscribe warship passage through the Turkish Straits. The Soviets appear to have now redesignated the KIEV class as some type of "aircraft carrying ship."

The Soviet Navy introduced several new and relatively radical cruiser and destroyer designs during the 1960s. At top is a KYNDA class cruiser with eight tubes for the long-range SS-N-3 antiship missile. The four-tube launchers are evident forward and aft of the ship's superstructure in this view. At center is a KASHIN class antiaircraft missile destroyer. This ship introduced gas turbine propulsion to large warships. At bottom is a KRESTA I class missile cruiser. The KRESTA I is a multi-mission ship, heavily armed and fitted with a variety of electronic systems.

The salient point to be understood with regard to Soviet aircraft carrier policy is that it appears that the Politburo has opted for yet another naval program which requires a long term commitment of extensive national resources and manpower. For whatever purpose or intent the Soviets pursue this high capital investment, the West cannot afford to ignore its future implications.

The KIEVs have an unusual design. They have a full load displacement of about 37,000 tons, are 900 feet long, have an angled flight deck some 600 feet long, and an island superstructure to starboard in the tradition of Western carriers. However, the forward part of these ships is similar to Soviet missile cruisers, with antiship, antisubmarine and antiaircraft missile launchers. They also have a profusion of more traditional weapons, electronic sensors, electronic warfare systems, and a number of advanced communications devices.

The lack of aircraft arresting wires and catapults on the flight deck limits the ships to helicopters and VSTOL aircraft. A mix of about 20 HORMONE helicopters, and 15 FORGER VTOL aircraft is a nominal air group, although this mix could be changed to meet varied mission requirements.

Although the primary mission of the KIEV class is stated by the Soviets as ASW, the ships also have a powerful antiship capability in their cruise missile battery. They have eight large launching tubes, with reloads for SS-N-12 missiles, which are an improvement over the older SS-N-3 antiship missiles. The HORMONE B helicopter has been seen aboard the KIEV class, with that helicopter being capable of providing over-the-horizon targeting information for the SS-N-12 missiles (which have a maximum range of some 300 nautical miles). Most of the embarked HORMONE helicopters are for ASW.

The FORGER has been observed operating in the antiship and nominal air defense roles. Depending on Soviet intentions, the aircraft might also be capable of ground attack, reconnaissance or other support roles. To date these aircraft have shown little inclination to stray any distance from the "Bird Farm". Tactical VSTOL technology is in its infancy with only FORGER and the British-designed HARRIER in service in significant numbers.* It is evident that this type of aircraft is destined to be widely deployed in a number of navies of the world. Although this first Soviet effort appears to be only VTOL capable and is relatively limited when compared to other front-line tactical aircraft, it is important to remember that it represents the beginnings of a most significant and growing trend in the Soviet Navy—sea-based, fixed-wing air power. As this power grows, the Soviet Navy will present opponents with a new range of threats, which in turn will tend to limit further those options available to Western naval commanders in a confrontation.

The KIEV is a second generation class of Soviet "aviation ship," following the helicopter carrier-missile cruisers MOSKVA and LENINGRAD, which were completed in 1967 and 1968, respectively. These earlier ships also were of innovative design, being essentially missile cruisers forward with a clear flight deck aft for operating up to 18 HORMONE antisubmarine helicopters. The latter ships are rated as "antisubmarine cruisers" by the Soviet Navy and have been used primarily in that role as well as serving as flagships.

Although helicopters are their main weapon, the MOSKVA class ships also have antiaircraft and antisubmarine missiles, ASW rockets, torpedo tubes, and guns. Advanced radars, sonars (both hull mounted and variable depth), and advanced electronic warfare equipment are fitted in the ships. They thus combine the full weapons-sensor suite of a guided missile cruiser with the capacity to handle a large squadron of ASW helicopters.

Cruisers

Late in 1962 the Soviets sent a new type of warship to sea, the first KYNDA class guided missile cruiser. This ship is of small cruiser size, displacing about 5,500 tons full load, and measuring 465 feet in length. The four KYNDA class ships are armed with antiaircraft missiles, multi-purpose guns, and antisubmarine weapons.

Most significant is the main battery of the KYNDAs: eight tubes for the SS-N-3 antiship cruise missile and eight reload missiles in the ship's superstructure. With a maximum operational range of some 250 nautical miles the SS-N-3 is one of the world's longest-range operational weapons of its kind for use against ships. To insure accuracy when fired at ranges beyond the horizon (about 25 miles), the SS-N-3 requires midcourse guidance. Still, the missile allows a Soviet warship, so equipped, to outrange every Allied warship except for an aircraft carrier. Thus, Admiral Gorshkov attempted to counter the U.S. superiority in aircraft carriers with another type of warship rather than compete in a category where the United States had overwhelming superiority.

*The HARRIER is flown by the Royal Air Force, with the AV-8A version in service with the U.S. Marine Corps and the Spanish Navy.

After producing the four KYNDA class ships, in 1967 Soviet yards began building the KRESTA I class of slightly larger dimensions (7,500 tons and 510 feet). In this ship, the Soviets reduced the number of long-range SS-N-3 launchers from eight to four, but increased the twin antiaircraft missile launchers from one to two, and added a helicopter hangar. This permits the KRESTA I to maintain a HORMONE helicopter on board to provide missile targeting or other services.

The KRESTA I was apparently an interim class, pending the final development of an ASW cruiser design, and only four ships were built. The next cruiser off the Soviet building ways was the slightly larger KRESTA II.

With the KRESTA II class the Soviets changed the main weapon from the long-range SS-N-3 to eight launchers for the SS-N-14 ASW missile with a range of about 25 miles. This missile change apparently reflected the Soviet shift in missions discussed earlier, from purely anticarrier to antisubmarine and selective sea control. In addition, the KRESTA II has improved antiaircraft missiles and more advanced electronics. Ten of the KRESTA II class ships were completed from 1970 to 1978.

Another new missile cruiser was introduced in 1973 with completion of the first ship of the KARA class. The size trend in surface warships continued, with this ship having a displacement of 9,700 tons and a length of about 570 feet. Again, there were improvements in weapon and sensor capabilities, and there also was a concomitant increase of operating range with the larger size, demonstrating the expanding horizons of Soviet maritime interests.

The Soviets' first nuclear powered surface warship, KIROV, on her initial sea trials in the Baltic in the summer of 1980. This ship is the largest combatant built in the world since World War II (excluding aircraft carriers). It carries 20 new type long-range cruise missiles, plus 12 vertical launch tubes for a new SAM system. This ship is equipped with numerous other weapons and sensors and is capable of carrying several helicopters aft.

The KRIVAK class missile frigate, also powered by gas turbines, is primarily an ASW ship. However, the KRIVAKs have torpedo tubes and guns, with later ships than the one seen here having two guns of 100mm caliber aft in place of the four 76mm AA weapons in twin gun mounts. These ships lack the helicopter facilities in contemporary U.S. destroyers and frigates.

The KARA class ships are gas turbine powered and have an armament similar to the KRESTA II class but with additional short-range antiaircraft missile launchers and a heavier gun battery. Seven KARA class cruisers are in service.

Besides the succeeding classes of missiles cruisers produced by the Soviet yards since the early 1960s, the Soviet Navy has retained twelve of the older SVERD-LOV class large cruisers built during the 1950s. Most of these ships remain in active service with an all-gun armament (12 six-inch guns). It is interesting to note that while almost all of the gun cruisers in the world's other navies have been retired, the Soviets continue to modernize and operate these ships.

One SVERDLOV class cruiser has a "refitted" twin launcher for medium-range antiaircraft missiles in place of a six-inch gun turret, while two other ships have been converted to "command ship" configurations. Amidships these two ships have been fitted with additional spaces for an admiral and his staff, satellite communications systems have been installed, and short-range missile launchers and rapid-fire "Gatling" guns are provided for antiaircraft/missile defense. These two modified SVERDLOVs, as well as the aviation ships, provide extensive communications, especially for command and control of operations. Several other SVERD-LOVs have recently been modernized as well, so the class is expected to remain in service for some years to come.

The Soviets are currently embarked on a most ambitious surface warship construction program. Four new classes of cruisers and large destroyers are now being built (compared to the U.S. Navy having only the TICONDEROGA-class Aegis guided-missile cruiser in production when this edition went to press).

The most impressive ship of this new generation of combatants is the Soviet's first nuclear powered warship. This ship, and a sister, are being built in Leningrad. Estimated to be some 28,000 full displacement tons, this will be the largest warship, apart from aircraft carriers, since World War II. The first of this class, KIROV, joined the fleet in late 1980. This ship carries 20 of a new type cruise missile of about the same size as the SS-N-12 but probably with improved performance. Additionally, the KIROV has 12 launchers for a new advanced surface-to-air missile system plus two shorter range SAM launchers, two 100mm guns, two ASW missile launchers, Gatling guns, torpedoe tubes, and several helicopters.

Still another Soviet cruiser, the 12,500-ton KRASINA was completed in 1983. This is primarily an antisurface cruiser, being fitted with 16 tubes for the large SS-N-12 missiles as well as antiair and antisubmarine weapons. The KRASINA represents a departure from the previous Soviet cruiser designs because of her lack of major ASW weapons. (The Soviet name for this class is SLAVA.)

Destroyers

Since World War II the Soviet Navy has experienced an evolutionary growth in the size and capability of destroyer-type warships.

The first post-World War II destroyer construction program produced the SKORYY class. Over 70 of these ships were built and a number still remain in active service. They are rarely seen beyond Soviet coastal waters. Fourteen of these ships have been transferred to Egypt, Poland, and Indonesia.

In the early 1950s and early 1960s the Soviet Navy successively introduced the KOTLIN class gun destroyer (27 built), the KILDIN class antiship missile destroyer (4 built), and the KRUPNYY class antiship missile destroyer (8 built). The KOTLINs have received various modifications over the years, including surface-to-air missiles added to nine (one since transferred to Poland). The KILDINs were built on KOTLIN hulls and three have also been modified in recent years, including the installation of four improved STYX antiship missiles. All eight of the KRUPNYYs have had their early antiship missile systems replaced by eight 57mm guns forward and a twin SAM launcher fitted aft, and additional ASW weapons and equipments were added. Thus reconfigured, these ships are now called the KANIN class.

From early 1963 through 1967 Soviet shipyards delivered 20 KASHIN class guided missile destroyers. These are ships of 4,500 tons and 476 feet in length. They are armed with two antiaircraft missile launchers, antisubmarine rocket launchers, five torpedo tubes, four 76mm multi-purpose guns, and mine rails. Five have been subsequently fitted with four short-range, antiship missiles (SS-N-2), and variable depth sonar. In the fall of 1974, one KASHIN class ship sank in the Black Sea, apparently as the result of an internal fire and explosion.

Their most distinctive feature is four large funnels in pairs for the tandem gas-turbine power plants. These were the world's first large warships with gas turbines and they give the KASHINs an estimated top speed of over 36 knots for brief periods.

Marine gas turbines provide a high horse-power-to-weight ratio, and are easy to maintain and replace. They can go from "cold-iron" to full power operations in a few minutes, and can rapidly accelerate, unlike steam turbines that require a steam buildup for acceleration.

Frigates

Soviet success with the KASHIN propulsion system led to gas turbine application in the small KRIVAK class frigates as well as the larger KARA class cruisers and UDALOY class destroyers.

After the KASHIN class the Soviets deferred the construction of destroyers for a full decade before beginning the UDALOY and SOVREMENNYY classes. These are both large ships, displacing in excess of 6,000 tons full load (i.e., the size of a KRESTA II class cruiser).

The UDALOY was completed in 1981, being a specialized antisubmarine ship. She has two SS-N-14 quad launchers, the large ASW weapon of the KRESTA II, KARA, KIROV, and KRIVAK classes. In addition, she carries two HELIX A

The SOVREMENNYY is lead ship for a destroyer class intended for the antiship role. She is armed with twin 130mm gun mounts forward and aft, the largest guns fitted in a Soviet warship since the 1950s. Her main armament is the SS-N-22 antiship missile, with a quad launcher on each side of the bridge structure.

antisubmarine helicopters, the first Soviet destroyer to have a helicopter hangar. The ship also has antiaircraft missiles, two 100mm guns, and other weapons.

The slightly smaller SOVREMENNYY, with the lead ship also completed in 1981, is a specialized antiship destroyer. The main weapons of this class are eight SS-N-22 antiship missiles. These ships also have a heavy gun armament, two 130mm twin turrets, plus antiaircraft missiles and antisubmarine weapons. An expandable helicopter hangar is provided so that a HORMONE B can be embarked to provide over-the-horizon targeting.

The Soviet Navy has a large number of frigates which operate with fleet formations on the high seas as antisubmarine escorts and as coastal patrol ships. The KRIVAK class missile frigate, the first of which went to sea in 1970, now numbers about 30 ships and construction continues. These ships displace about 3,600 tons and have an overall length of 405 feet. The KRIVAKs are armed with both antisubmarine and antiaircraft missiles. They have a four-tube launcher for the SS-N-14 ASW missiles and two twin reloadable launchers for the SA-N-4 short-range SAM missile. In addition, the ship has antisubmarine rockets, eight torpedo tubes, mine rails, and four 76mm guns. In some of the later ships two single guns of 100mm size replace the 76mm weapon; these ships have been designated the KRIVAK II class. The ship's sensors are complemented by advanced electronic systems, including both hull-mounted and variable depth sonars. The KRIVAKs have been built at a rate of three to four per year.

With more than 30 KRIVAKs in service, construction continues. Although the Soviets have developed a new light frigate, the 1,900-ton KONI, only one is in Soviet service, apparently a training and demonstration ship with series production intended for foreign navies. (The KONI class has been transferred to Algeria, Cuba, East Germany, and Yugoslavia.)

The remainder of the approximately 175 frigates in the Soviet Navy are smaller ships of the MIRKA, PETYA, GRISHA, and RIGA classes. The first three classes are some 1,200 to 1,600 tons, particularly suited for coastal ASW and related defense missions. There are 30 some of the older RIGA class, completed in the 1950s, and of limited combat value.

Beyond the KRIVAK and KONI classes, only the GRISHA appears to remain in production.

Although these frigates are smaller than most Western frigates, they nonetheless deploy regularly to the Mediterranean and Indian Ocean where they are an integral part of the permanent Soviet squadrons operating in those seas.

B. Small Combatants

The Soviet Union operates large numbers of small combatants—missile, torpedo, patrol, and mine craft.

Probably the most publicized of these craft are the OSA missile boats which displace some 215 tons and are 129 feet long. Each OSA carries four launchers for the SS-N-2 STYX missile, which has a range of

A NATYA class ocean minesweeper. The Soviets operate almost 400 mine warfare ships and craft as well as maintain what is estimated to be by far the world's largest stockpile of mines.

about 25 miles. The OSA II boats carry improved missiles which have a range of over 40 miles. With a sustained speed of 34 knots and two rapid-fire, twin 30mm gun mounts, the OSAs are potent ship killers. About 120 OSAs are currently in Soviet service and over 125 have been transferred to other navies (as have some 60 of the earlier, two-missile KOMAR missile boats).

In 1969 the Soviets introduced the NANUCHKA class guided missile patrol combatant into service. This ship displaces amost 900 tons and is 194 feet long. The NANUCHKA I has a twin SA-N-4 anti-aircraft missile launcher forward and a twin 57mm gun aft. A later variant, the NANUCHKA III, have a single 57mm and a 30mm Gatling gun. The main battery consists of six tubes for the SS-N-9 missile. This antiship weapon has a maximum range estimated at about 60 miles. Several modified versions of this ship, NANUCHKA II, carrying four SS-N-2 missiles have been sold to India.

A new hydrofoil missile boat, the SARANCHA, has been operating for several years. This gas turbine powered craft is smaller than the NANUCHKA and mounts only four SS-N-9 missiles, plus an SA-N-4 missile system and a Gatling gun.

Besides the aforementioned ships, the Soviet Navy has large numbers of a variety of classes of small combatants: patrol boats, torpedo boats, hydrofoil patrol boats, submarine chasers, gunboats, and river monitors. The maritime arm of the KGB

BABOCHKA class PCSH. A gas turbine powered, hydrofoil, sub chaser which is just entering the Soviet inventory. This boat appears to be armed with a number of torpedos plus two "Gatling" guns. As with larger surface warships the Soviets are producing a number of new classes of smaller combatants.

(the state security police) also operates several classes of frigates and small combatants.

Several new classes of these types of ships have been observed and include the MATKA class missile equipped hydrofoil gunboat, the TARANTUL missile gunboat, and the BABOUCHKA class submatine chaser.

The Soviet Navy's mine warfare force is the largest in the world. Over 200 ocean and coastal mine-sweepers, plus a number of minesweeping boats, make up the active force. The classes of ocean minesweepers (540 to 900 tons) includes the NATYA, YURKA, and T-43 classes; and the coastal minesweepers (200 to 400 tons) include the SONYA, ZHENYA, VANYA, and SASHA classes.

TURYA class PTH. The hydrofoil torpedo boats are armed with four torpedo tubes, a twin 57mm dual purpose gun aft, and a quad 23mm mount forward. These boats usually operate in the littoral seas of the USSR.

The Soviet Navy uses these mine warfare ships for a variety of tasks besides their primary function, such as patrol and picket duties. Besides this large force of minewarfare ships, it is estimated the Soviets also maintain the world's largest stock of mines of numerous different types. The Russians have a long history of interest in mine warfare and continue to actively pursue all aspects of mining, both offensively and defensively.

C. Submarines

The Soviet Navy long has been a world leader in operating submarines. Beginning in the late 1930s, the Soviet Navy generally has had more undersea craft than any other navy.

Today the Soviet submarine force numbers about 360 units. In discussing them one must address three specific categories:

- Torpedo attack submarines—that attack an enemy surface warship or submarine using torpedoes or missile delivered ASW weapons.
- Cruise missiles submarines—that fire large antiship cruise missiles as well as torpedoes.
- Strategic ballistic missile submarines—armed with vertically-launched, nuclear-tipped missiles for strategic targets.

The Soviet Navy is operating a total of about 165 nuclear powered submarines compared to some 115 in the U.S. Navy.

Attack Submarines

The Soviet Navy operates about 210 attack submarines. Some 60 are nuclear-powered of the ALFA, VICTOR, ECHO I, and NOVEMBER classes. The ALFA, with a speed of 43 knots, is the world's fastest undersea craft and the world's deepest diving. The improved VICTOR III is also in production. This 30-knot-plus craft has a towed ar-

Aircraft and submarines armed with cruise missiles are the principal antiship forces of the Soviet Navy. At top is a CHARLIE I class submarine which has eight submerged-launched SS-N-7 missiles and, below, an ECHO II with eight SS-N-3 missiles fired from the surface. Both of these classes are nuclear powered and can operate in virtually any ocean area.

ray passive sonar as well as other advanced features. Two new attack submarine designs will become operational in the mid-1980s.

The Soviets continue to produce diesel-electric attack submarines with the TANGO, introduced in 1972, and the KILO, 1982, are in series production. The older but highly capable FOXTROT remains in production for foreign navies (Cuba, India, and Libya, with other nations expected to follow).

Soviet officials have noted that diesel-electric submarines offer a quiet-running, highly capable platform that can operate in shallower waters than the larger, nuclear submarines, and at a small fraction of the nuclear submarine construction and operating costs.

The prime weapons of these attack submarines are antisubmarine and antiship torpedoes; however, mines also can be carried. The newer submarines have a rocket-propelled ASW weapon as well.

Cruise Missile Submarines

Building on German experiments during World War II, both the U.S. and Soviet navies experimented with missile-launching submarines after World War II. In the U.S. Navy this effort evolved into the REGULUS cruise missile program. Although the REGULUS could be used against ships, the lack of significant Soviet surface threat in the 1950s led to American development of the REGULUS as a strategic weapon for strikes against bases, ports and cities. The POLARIS technology quickly overtook the REGULUS in this role.

The Soviet Navy developed cruise missile submarines in the 1950s for strategic attack and as a part of a strategy to counter U.S. aircraft carriers. Initially, existing submarines were converted to fire the long-range SS-N-3 missile. Then, newer submarines designed to carry the SS-N-3 joined the Soviet fleet —the diesel powered JULIETT class and the nuclear powered ECHO I and II classes.

After producing about 50 submarines of the JULI-ETT and ECHO classes, the Soviets completed the first CHARLIE I class SSGN in 1968 with the improved CHARLIE II following several years later. These nuclear powered submarines can fire eight antiship cruise missiles while remaining submerged at a range of some 30 miles from an intended target. Although the CHARLIE missile range is less than that of submarines armed with the SS-N-3, the latter submarines must surface before firing their missiles. The underwater launch capability of the CHARLIE makes this craft one of the most potent antiship submarines in service today. All of these cruise missile submarines also have standard torpedo tubes.

The Soviets' newest cruise missile submarine is the large OSCAR class. With the lead submarine completed in 1982, this is the largest attack-cruise missile undersea craft yet built, with a submerged displacement of about 14,000 tons. The OSCAR is a fast, 30-knot submarine carrying 24 SS-N-19 missiles, the same weapon in the KIROV class cruiser. This missile combines the features of underwater launch with long range (over 250 nautical miles) and has a large warhead.

The Soviet Navy's cruise missile submarines and their missile-armed bombers form the greatest threat to Allied naval forces operating on the high seas. This is especially so when within range of Soviet air bases where the Soviets can launch coordinated attacks using not only reconnaissance aircraft to provide target data for submarine-launched missiles, but also their extensive force of naval and air force missile equipped bombers.

The 34 YANKEE class strategic missile submarines completed since 1967 were the "second generation" Soviet SSBNs. More than 30 later DELTA I/II/III submarines are now at sea, with some sources indicating a still more advanced SSBN, the TYPHOON class, also being under construction. An intensive submarine missile development effort has accompanied their construction.

Ballistic Missile Submarines

The development of nuclear weapons led to another role for the submarine, that of strategic or ballistic missile attack against land targets. Submarines are valuable in this role because the difficulty of their detection in the ocean depths makes them highly survivable against hostile attack.

As discussed earlier, the Soviets began converting existing diesel powered submarines in the mid-1950s to fire short-range Submarine Launched Ballistic Missiles (SLBMs). Then, in the early 1960s, the GOLF class diesel and HOTEL class nuclear SLBM submarines were completed. These submarines were initially limited by mechanical difficulties, short-range missiles, and the requirement for surfacing to launch their missiles. (Most of these submarines were later provided with a submerged missile launch capability and improved weapons.)

Today, the Soviet Navy has an SLBM force that exceeds that of the U.S. Navy in numbers of submarines and in missiles. By the end of 1974, the Soviet Navy had 34 of the YANKEE class SSBNs in service, each carrying 16 nuclear-tipped missiles with a range of at least 1,300 nautical miles (later increased to about 1,600 miles). During 1973 the first of the larger DELTA class submarines was completed. The early DELTAs displace some 11,000 tons submerged and have an overall length of about 460 feet. The DELTA I has 12 tubes for the SS-N-8 missile with an estimated range of over 4,000 nautical miles. The DELTA II and III carries 16 SS-N-8 or SS-N-18 SLBMs, respectively, and are about 50 feet longer than the DELTA I.

The SS-N-18 missile is the first Soviet SLBM to have multiple independently targeted re-entry vehicles (MIRV), carrying as many as seven warheads that can be aimed at separate targets. The SS-N-18 is more accurate if not longer ranged than the SS-N-8. The SS-N-17 is the first solid-propellant SLBM developed by the Soviets but only one converted YANKEE has been observed with this missile. The SS-N-17 uses a post-boost vehicle that would allow it to carry a MIRV package. This missile probably has increased accuracy and range compared to the SS-N-6 carried in the YANKEEs.

To keep within the SALT I limits of 62 strategic missile submarines, the Soviets are now decommissioning older YANKEE class submarines, with some having been converted to attack/cruise missile configurations.

The Soviets have had to decommission these older YANKEEs because of the continued construction of the large (13,000 ton) DELTA III class and development of the subsequent, gigantic

TYPHOON class. At about 25,000 tons submerged displacement, the TYPHOON is the largest undersea craft ever built. (In comparison, the U.S. TRIDENT missile submarines are 18,700 tons submerged.)

The TYPHOON submarine actually has two inner submarine hulls within a large outer hull. There are tubes *forward* of the sail structure for 20 SS-N-20 ballistic missiles, four less than in the U.S. TRIDENT submarines. The Soviet weapons are reported to have MIRV warheads as well as sufficient range to enable them to reach most if not all U.S. cities from Soviet ports or from beneath the polar ice pack.

In addition to the OSCAR and DELTA III strategic missile submarines, the Soviets appear to have eight other classes in production—two new SSGN designs, the OSCAR, ALFA, VICTOR III, KILO, TANGO, and FOXTROT. At this time the only U.S. submarines in production are the OHIO class TRIDENT missile class and the LOS ANGELES attack class.

D. Aircraft

Soviet Naval Aviation (SNA) is completely subordinate to the Soviet Navy, with regiments being assigned to each of the four fleets under an aviation officer who reports directly to the fleet commander. This naval air arm consists of over 1,500 aircraft, most of which are based ashore. Helicopters are carried in several cruiser and destroyer classes, including the aviation ships MOSKVA and LENINGRAD, and VTOL aircraft as well as helicopters fly from the KIEV class carriers.

Although they are career naval officers, aviators in the Soviet Navy have the same rank structure as the Soviet Air Force, which also provides their basic training.

Soviet naval aviation currently has four basic missions:

Reconnaissance and Surveillance

Naval aircraft are employed in long-range reconnaissance ("recce") and ocean surveillance, with some aircraft equipped to provide mid-course target data for antiship missiles launched "over the horizon" from surface ships, submarines, and other aircraft. Reconnaissance aircraft now in use include about 50 of the larger BEAR D turbo-prop planes;

The Soviet Navy flies over 500 twin-jet BADGER aircraft in the missile strike, reconnaissance, electronic, tanker, and training roles. This BADGER was photographed while looking over a U.S. carrier. With the BADGER is a U.S. Navy F-4 PHANTOM fighter.

about 100 twin-jet BADGER aircraft, with about the same performance as the now-discarded U.S. B-47 jet bombers; and a few BLINDER jet aircraft that have a supersonic dash speed. Additionally, the MAY maritime patrol aircraft are used for surveillance and reconnaissance missions.

These aircraft and others flown by SNA are described in Appendix D.

Antiship Strike

The prime striking force of Soviet Naval Aviation consists of some 370 strike aircraft. There are almost 100 of the twin-jet BACKFIRE bombers, a supersonic aircraft that is also flown, like other SNA bombers, by Soviet strategic aviation (formerly designated Long-Range Aviation).

The largest number of bombers in SNA are BADGERS, an older twin-jet aircraft, with more than 200 of the C and G missile strike aircraft being in service as well as about 25 BADGER A aircraft carrying free-fall bombs. SNA also has perhaps 40 BLINDER, three-jet supersonic bombers that carry free-fall bombs. The BADGER A and BLINDER bombers would be useful in conflicts supporting amphibious operations and against merchant shipping.

The more than 300 missile-armed BACKFIRE and BADGER aircraft carry the AS-4 antiship missile. This "stand-off" missile has a range up to

250 nautical miles, and can dive on its target at high supersonic speed carrying a conventional warhead of some 2,200 pounds or a nuclear weapon.

In the offing is the more capable BLACKJACK, a four-engine, long-range strike aircraft that will be flown by the Navy as well as strategic aviation. And, more-capable antiship missiles are under development.

Beyond these naval aircraft armed with antiship weapons, certain BEAR and BADGER bombers of

A FORGER VTOL fighter sits on the deck of the carrier KIEV. Note intake panel behind cockpit which covers the lift engines when the aircraft is in horizontal flight.

Soviet strategic aviation can be employed in attacks against shipping. Most of these aircraft can be refueled in flight from the Navy's 75 tankers, as can naval strike aircraft. Strategic aviation also has a small number of tanker aircraft.

Fighter-Attack

The introduction of aircraft carriers and the FORGER aircraft give the SNA another dimension of capability. The FORGER can be fitted with a variety of short-range missiles, rockets, or bombs for use against shore or ship targets, and can intercept hostile patrol and ASW aircraft.

The land-based FITTER fighter-bomber has been introduced into SNA during the past several years, providing the Baltic and subsequently the Pacific fleets with antiship strike and close support for amphibious operations.

The nuclear-propelled aircraft carrier now under construction in the U.S.S.R. is expected to have conventional fixed-wing aircraft, providing the Soviet fleet with high-performance aircraft based at sea. In the interim, the FORGER VTOL has been useful in the development of sea-based tactical aviation tactics, doctrine, and support.

Antisubmarine

The Soviet Navy has a large force of fixed-wing aircraft and helicopters configured for submarine detection and attack. This force currently includes about 30 ASW configured BEAR F aircraft, 50 MAY turbo-prop aircraft that resemble the U.S. P-3 ORI-ON, and 100 MAIL twin-engine flying boat aircraft. Only the BEAR F appears to be still in production. These aircraft operate from Soviet land bases to search out seaward areas for foreign submarines. They carry a variety of detection equipment as well as ASW depth bombs and torpedoes.

An increasing number of antisubmarine helicopters are being flown by the Soviet Navy. The HOR-MONE A, a twin turboshaft helicopter, is flown from the newer Soviet cruisers, as well as from the helicopter carriers MOSKVA and LENINGRAD and the KIEV class aircraft carriers. An ASW version of the HIP helicopter, which has been named the HAZE by Western intelligence, has been entering SNA inventory. Because of its larger size, it is unlikely to be used on existing Soviet warships. It is more likely a replacement for the older shore-based, HOUND ASW helicopters. The HAZE is reported to be now operating in all four fleets.

A long-awaited successor to the HORMONE, the larger HELIX is now flying in the ASW role. The helicopter strongly resembles the HORMONE but has a twin vice triple rudder configuration.

The KIEV class carriers operate between 14 and 17 HORMONE and HELIX helicopters, most for ASW, but some HORMONE B models for targeting antiship missiles. A few HORMONE C utility helicopters are found in the fleet, being used for a variety of support activities.

Support

Soviet Naval Aviation also operates some 375 transport, training, and utility aircraft of various types. Although basic and some advanced training

An AIST class air cushion vehicle provides high speed across the beach assault for Soviet Naval Infantry. The Soviet Navy is by far the world's largest operator of surface effect ships. There are currently three different classes of air cushion vehicles in the naval inventory—the AIST is the largest.

are provided by the Soviet Air Forces, naval operational and "transition" training is accomplished within the Navy.

The SNA retains a number of transports to meet the high-priority passenger and cargo requirements of naval headquarters and the fleet.

In recent years Soviet Naval Aviation has been gaining in strength and in prestige. Approximately 68,000 officers and enlisted men are assigned to SNA, about 15 percent of the Navy's strength (including the Naval Infantry and Coastal Defense forces). While much smaller than the U.S. naval air arm, SNA is increasing in capability and provides the Soviet Navy with improved effectiveness. The production rate of BACKFIREs, the new BLACK-JACK strike aircraft, the KIEV and follow-on carrier classes, and other developments will continue to improve this segement of the Soviet fleet.

E. Amphibious Forces

Another area of continuing development in the Soviet Navy has been amphibious assault forces. Within the Soviet Navy, "marines" are known as "naval infantry." Since it was reformed in the early 1960s, this force has received considerable publicity in the Soviet press and is bannered as an elite combat force. Today there are an estimated 13,000 Soviet marines, mostly allocated to the four fleets. (The U.S. Marine Corps, by comparison, numbers about 185,000 men and women.)

The mission of the Soviet marines and hence their organization and equipment differ somewhat from that of the U.S. Marine Corps. The Soviets are not able to conduct extensive independent operations as our marines are. Instead, they spearhead amphibious landings for other ground forces and hold captured beachheads against counterattack, carry out "prolonged" river crossings and defend naval bases.

Although described as "light" infantry, the Soviet marine force is highly mechanized and is equipped with tracked and wheeled amphibious vehicles, including tanks and armored personnel carriers.

Amphibious lift for the naval infantry is provided primarily by IVAN ROGOV class LPDs, ALLIGATOR class and ROPHUCHA class LSTs, and POLNOCNY class LSMs. The Soviet amphibious forces exercise regularly in their respective fleet areas and regularly deploy to the Mediterranean, off West Africa, and the Indian Ocean. The Soviet Navy has about 30 LSTs and over 50 LSMs,

plus numerous lesser landing craft and air cushion vehicles for amphibious operations.

The Soviet Navy is now the world's largest operator of military air cushion vehicles for which development continues. There are three classes currently in use: The GUS, LEBED and large AIST class.

Although small by comparison to the U.S. Marine Corps (the Soviet Naval Infantry is the second largest marine force in the world), the potential power of even a few hundred Soviet marines afloat in any given area during a crisis provides the Soviet Union with a valuable politico-military tool. For operations at some distance from the U.S.S.R., the Soviet ability to conduct an amphibious assault is limited to landings against positions where little or no opposition is expected ashore or in the seaward approaches of the landing area. But the Soviets have in hand, or are developing, the elements necessary to provide a formidable projection into distant waters, if that is their choice. These include the improvement in assault lift capability, the expansion of a large administrative lift ability designed into certain ships of the Merchant Marine, the retention of a substantial gunfire support strength in the older cruisers and destroyers, development of sea-based tactical air power, and a steadily improving underway replenishment capability. The Soviet Navy's ability to project tactical power ashore at some distance from the Soviet littoral may be part of Admiral Gorshkov's "grand plan" in achieving a "balanced fleet".

F. Auxiliaries

As befitting a fleet of its size, the Soviet Navy operates a large number of auxiliaries, including many types and classes performing a myriad of function in various roles. The total of all categories approximates 760 ships.

One area in which the Soviets have lagged behind the Western navies is that of underway replenishment. The Soviets provide the great percentage of replenishment and routine maintenance to their deployed units in open anchorages in international waters. Although such activities appear more than adequate in peacetime operations, this mode of support would be most vulnerable in times of conflict. The Soviet Navy has slowly been improving their capabilities in the area of underway replenishment. Today, of 80 replenishment ships about 20 are capable of alongside refueling. The BORIS CHILIKIN class AORs and the new BEREZINA AOR are the most capable of these types. The Soviets still extensively use the astern method of refueling, which requires the participants to proceed at slow speed or remain dead in the water. The Soviets also rely on the merchant marine to provide a substantial percentage of their fuel at sea.

BEREZINA is a 40,000 ton multi-purpose replenishment ship, similar in size, appearance and capabilities to our WICHITA class AORs. It is armed with guns and missiles and appears to be designed to operate as an integral part of a battle group. Besides various liquids, this ship can also transfer solid stores, including missiles, while underway. The ship has a two helicopter hangar capacity. Although only one of this class has been built, it is expected the Soviets will continue to develop and improve this type of auxiliary.

Other auxiliaries which deploy regularly are material and fleet support ships such as: large submarine tenders (AS), which also serve the fleet as command and general maintenance ships, missile tenders (AEM), water transports (AW), (many Soviet ships suffer from small fresh water evaporator capacity), stores ships (AF), repair ships (AR), ocean tugs (ATA), etc. In addition to auxiliaries providing direct support to the fleet, other auxiliaries of the Soviet Navy are plying the "seven seas" in virtually every corner of the world in any

given day. These include such types as intelligence, survey and research, and space event support ships.

The Soviets also use auxiliaries extensively for fleet maintenance and support in many of their home operating bases, in lieu of extensive fixed base assets ashore.

The Soviets rely to a fair extent on their Warsaw Pact allies, particularly Poland and East Germany to construct naval auxiliaries. A more recent example of this is the building of two large hospital ships in Poland; the Soviets have not had any such ships for years. The reasons the Soviets feel they need such ships at this juncture are speculative. Finland, West Germany, Sweden, Japan and the United Kingdom have also built auxiliaries now serving in the Soviet Navy.

G. Surveillance, Intelligence, and Communications

The Soviet Navy's increased operations have been matched by quantitative and by qualitative increases in related surveillance, intelligence, and communications activities. The most obvious manifestation of this aspect of Soviet naval activity has

The newest class replenishment ship (AOR) is the 40,000 ton BEREZINA. This large ship is equipped to move both liquids and solids while steaming alongside either to port or starboard. It also carries two helicopters for vertical replenishment of stores and personnel. This ship is armed with a twin launcher SA-N-4 SAM and two twin 57mm guns.

been the extensive operations of passive intelligence collection or "spy" ships.

These ships are known as "intelligence collectors" and are designated as AGIs; more than 50 of them are in service. They are often depicted in the press as disguised fishing trawlers. However, they are clearly identifiable as naval intelligence ships, manned by naval personnel, flying the Soviet naval ensign, and easily identified by their varied and unusual electronic antennas. Some of the AGIs are of modified trawler design, others of modified survey-research ship design, and a number are built-for-the-purpose of intelligence "factories." The latter of the PRIMORYE class displace about 4,000 tons. A new large AGI, the BALZAM class, joined the Soviet fleet in 1980—this ship displaces over 5,000 tons.

Soviet AGI-type ships normally keep watch off the U.S. missile submarine bases of Holy Loch, Scotland, and Guam in the Marianas. An AGI normally operates off the Southeastern coast of the United States, a position that permits surveillance of the submarine bases at Charleston, South Carolina, or Kings Bay, Georgia; the aircraft carrier operating areas off Virginia or Florida; or the missile activity at Cape Kennedy. AGIs regularly dog NATO and U.S. naval forces during exercises and are usually present in most Soviet-United States naval confrontations.

The concept of operating ships exclusively for overt intelligence tasks was discarded by the U.S. Navy after the misfortunes of the USS PUEBLO (captured by the North Koreans) and the USS LIBERTY (severely damaged by Israeli air and naval attack back in the 1960s). Significantly, U.S. Navy ships employed in this passive intelligence role during that period were converted World War II-built cargo ships, whereas the Soviet vessels are of relatively recent construction. Over the last several years, the Soviets have armed a number of their AGIs with small surface-to-air missiles.

In addition to AGIs, the Soviet Navy, like other major navies, employs surface warships, submarines and aircraft for intelligence collection.

Increasingly, the Soviet Navy is also employing advanced satellite surveillance systems. Recent naval-associated surveillance satellites have improved collection rates and processing capabilities. These include electronic intelligence (ELINT) satellites (that can "lock on" to electronic signals from Western warships to provide location information), radar surveillance satellites and photographic satellites. The ELINT and radar satellites can provide almost real-time detection and possibly some weapon-

guidance capability.

Satellite surveillance systems are in extensive use by the Soviet armed forces. According to published reports, the Soviets apparently employed reconnaissance satellites to keep track of the 1973 war in the Middle East. Four reconnaissance satellites were orbited during the 12-day period in early October, apparently related to the Arab-Israeli war that erupted on October 6, 1973. Indications are that the Soviets increased their satellite collection during the more recent Iranian and Afghan crises.

Satellites are also employed by the Soviet Navy for long-range communications. A number of Soviet warships and support ships have satellite communication equipment, including the KIEV-class carriers and the two SVERDLOV class cruisers that were modified to serve as command and communication ships in remote ocean areas. These ships are fitted with advanced communications equipment, command and control spaces, and accommodations for an admiral and staff. More recently the Soviets modified at least GOLF class submarines for this same purpose.

The Soviet Navy has developed advanced conventional communication equipment for the tactical coordination of strike forces. For example, Soviet surface missile ships, missile-armed submarines, and aircraft are able to rapidly exchange targeting information and coordinate strikes against surface ship targets. During the large-scale OKEAN maneuvers of 1970 and 1975, the Soviets were observed to simulate several coordinated attacks against surface ships. In some phases of the multi-ocean exercise, naval bombers simultaneously flew simulated strike missions in both the North Atlantic and Western Pacific Oceans, with warships in the different oceans being attacked at the same moment. Now the Soviets conduct more extensive and complex exercises than in the past, particularly during the spring and summer periods.

This requirement for simultaneous strikes in widely separated ocean areas is part of the Soviet Navy's "short war" or "first salvo" concept discussed earlier in this publication.

Published Soviet reports describing OKEAN 1970 tell of the Navy Commander-in-Chief being able to communicate with major units anywhere in the world almost instantly, knowing that an order had been executed by a ship in a "matter of minutes," having available in real time the status of air, surface, and underwater situations, including friendly and enemy orders of battle, and being able to monitor "how the (ship) commander conducts a search and accurately judges the effectiveness of his actions."

H. Other Warsaw Pact Navies

Four of the six non-Soviet Warsaw Pact (NSWP) countries have navies: Poland, the German Democratic Republic (GDR) (East Germany), Bulgaria and Rumania. These forces are designed primarily to operate in the coastal areas of their respective countries, and units are seldom seen outside of the Baltic Sea (Poland and the GDR) or the Black Sea (Bulgaria and Rumania).

The Baltic NSWP navies are by far the more capable in relation to those in the Black Sea, and it appears the former are much more integrated with the Soviet Navy in matters of Warsaw Pact operations than the latter. These navies have a proliferation of ship classes that are home-built or provided by the Soviets.

The Poles and Germans are excellent ship builders, and their navies have several classes of ships which are of indigenous design and construction. Examples of these are the FROSH class LST, LIBELLE class PTL and HAI class PG in the GDR Navy and the POLNOCNY class LSM and the OBLUZE class PCS in the Polish Navy. A number of amphibious ships and auxiliaries in the Soviet Navy were also built in Poland.

The Poles have a naval air arm which consists of about 90 helicopters, older MIG fighters and BEAGLE bombers. The GDR Navy operates a small contingent of ASW helicopters.

Poland has a well balanced navy which includes: four WHISKEY class submarines; a KOTLIN class DDG; a number of smaller combatants, including OSA class missile boats; a good size amphibious force; about 50 mine warfare ships and craft, plus a few auxiliaries. Although there are no marines in the Polish Navy, there is a dedicated "amphibious landing division" in the Polish Army which exercises with the navy's amphibious assault force.

The GDR Navy has no submarines or destroyers but does have two of the new KONI class frigates recently built by the Soviets. They also operate a large coastal patrol force including OSA class missile boats, an amphibious force able to lift the amphibious dedicated motorized rifle regiment in the GDR Army, and a coastal minesweeper group.

The Rumanian Navy consists mainly of 3 POTI class patrol escorts, about 66 coastal patrol craft, including a few OSAs, and a mine warfare force of approximately 32. Some of the Rumanian units were purchased from Communist China, another indication that the Rumanians do not collaborate as closely with the Soviets as the latter might wish.

The Bulgarian Navy has four submarines of the WHISKEY and ROMEO classes, two RIGA class frigates, three POTI class patrol escorts, a mine warfare force of 26, and about 24 coastal combatants, including several OSA missile boats.

A BALZAM-class intelligence collection ship (AGI) playing her trade. There are several of these 5,000-ton ships in service, built especially for the AGI role. Like many other AGIs, the BALZAMs have short-range antiaircraft missiles.

NAVAL WEAPONS

The ADMG-630 Gatling-Action 6-Barrel 30-mm AA gun is replacing the older twin 30-mm on most Soviet Naval Combatants for close-in defense against ASCM.

The quad SS-N-14 antisubmarine missile launcher on a KRESTA II missile cruiser. This weapon carries a homing torpedo to a range of about 25nm.

The twin 57mm dual purpose gun of an ASW frigate. This is a fully automatic water-cooled gun system.

The twin SS-N-3 cruiser missile launcher on the KRESTA I missile cruiser. The launcher is hydraulic elevated to the firing position in this view.

The 152mm (6 inch) triple gun turrets on a SVERDLOV class cruiser. Although these ships are now approaching 30 years of age the Soviets still actively maintain them as flagships and shore bombardment platforms.

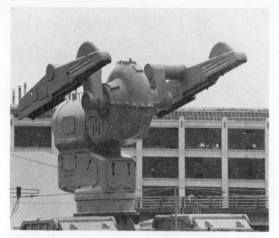

The SA-N-1 GOA missile launcher on a Soviet destroyer. The Soviets consider this a dual-purpose, antiship and antiaircraft weapon.

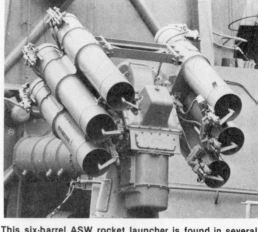

This six-barrel ASW rocket launcher is found in several classes of Soviet surface warships. Their range is several thousand meters.

Twin 76mm dual-purpose gun mounts, as in this KARA class cruiser, are fitted in several cruiser, destroyer, and frigate classes.

Twin 30mm rapid-fire guns, as shown here, and multi-barrel "Gatling" guns are fitted in Soviet ships for close-in defense.

The after section of a KARA-class missile cruiser shown here reveals the ship's ten torpedo tubes for ASW or antiship torpedoes, the SA-N-3 GOBLET missile launcher, and, along-side the hangar, RBU-1000 ASW rocket launchers.

49

Section 5. Soviet Naval Personnel

However technically perfect the Navy may be, man is always the basis of naval forces, the ruler of all the weapons of warfare.

Admiral of the Fleet of the Soviet Union
S.G. GORSHKOV

The officers and men of the Soviet Navy occupy a respected position within Soviet society. Military service in the Soviet Union is characterized as a special form of service to the State and is rewarded by a continuous deluge of praise and commendation from Soviet public leaders and the press. The Navy is also given a special place of respect in Soviet eyes due to its close association with the revolution and connections with the Party, the 1921 Kronshradt rebellion notwithstanding. Finally, even more tantalizing to the average Soviet citizen, for whom travel to a distant foreign place is a virtual impossibility, is the opportunity which the navyman has to see the world in some of the most modern warships afloat.

The enlisted men are either two-year or three-year draftees; the latter term of service is required if the conscript is assigned sea duty. The Soviety Union does not draft women for military service. They are employed in clerical and support positions, and are not considered an integral part of the armed services as are service women of the United States.

Of approximately 461,000 uniformed personnel in the Soviet Navy, about 186,000 serve in ships and 68,000 are attached to naval aviation. In addition to the 13,000 man Naval Infantry force, another 14,000 are assigned to Coastal Defense activities, about 57,000 are engaged in various stages of training, and 123,000 are used to provide shore support. Additionally, a large number of civilians, perhaps as many as 30,000, form the crews of the majority of Soviet naval auxiliary ships.

A. Pre-Service Training

The 1967 Law of Universal Military Service provides for draft eligibility at age 18 and naval service of three years (two years if serving ashore, a term which is comparable to that of the other armed services).

Pre-induction military training in the Soviet Union is under the control of the local military commission which organizes and administers the program. For those enrolled in the normal ten-year school program or a vocational technical school, military training is conducted in school during the 9th and 10th grades. Students who finish their education at the 8th grade level receive military training at their place of employment. This military training is a 140-hour program over a two-year period which includes military indoctrination, schooling in basic military skills, and weapons instruction.

In addition to compulsory training, paramilitary clubs and military specialist preparation courses are conducted by the DOSAAF (All-Union Voluntary Society for Assistance to the Army, Air Force, and Navy). DOSAAF clubs and specialist courses are frequently oriented toward a particular service. The more general clubs prepare the inductee for military service, usually in the army, while specific courses are designed to provide the specialized training that would otherwise be conducted while the conscript was in the service. Thus, there are Navy clubs which teach sailing and seamanship, as well as the more intensive and specific courses for radio operators, helmsmen, and divers. This training not only aids the military in reducing in-service instruction time, but also offers to Soviet youth opportunities to participate in activities which are denied to other members of Soviet society.

Taken at face value, these pre-draft and paramilitary programs appear quite formidable. On the other hand, the Soviet press periodically voices relatively strong criticism of their quality. Nevertheless, even a broad brush introduction to military training and the attendant physical exercise must ease the burden of military preparation. Further, some DOSAAF-trained specialists, usually in the less technically demanding disciplines can adequately fulfill their fleet assignments without further specialist training.

Upon completion of their active navy duty the conscripts, about 130,000 yearly, are retained on the reserve lists until they are 50 years of age. This provides a large pool of semi-trained manpower, especially those men who are only four or five years removed from their active service.

B. Enlisted Men

The enlisted man of the Soviet Navy is a conscript with limited training and little career inclination. Conscripts are drawn from all the 16 republics within the U.S.S.R., and often those from Asian republics speak little Russian. Since conscripts are inducted into the services twice a year, this means that every six months about 15 percent of the naval enlisted strength is replaced by recruits.

Basic Training

The new inductee undergoes a nine-week basic training program, after which he is either sent to a specialist school or directly to a duty assignment. A small number of recruits that have previously completed a DOSAAF specialty are sent directly to sea duty from basic training, while those judged physically or intellectually substandard are assigned to shore duty (as librarians, storekeepers, etc.). Approximately 75 percent of the men entering the Navy undergo specialist training, after which they receive their first shipboard assignment.

Specialist Training

Soviet technical training is of four to six months' duration. Specialists graduate with an apparent understanding of the theoretical complexities of their own specialty but with little practical training. Consequently, the more significant and practical training for the enlisted man is received after he arrives on board ship.

Once aboard, the enlisted man will be assigned to a more senior sailor who, along with the officers and warrant officers in his department, will train him as his replacement. The new specialist then begins his study for a class specialist rating of Master 1, 2, or 3. If a sailor passes his Master 3 specialist test, fulfills certain requirements of the Party youth organization (Komsomol), and has no disciplinary violations, he will be rated "outstanding" by his ship's captain. The number and class of specialists and the number rated outstanding is considered a significant measure in evaluating a ship's perfor-

mance. It is not surprising, therefore, that over 90 percent of all seamen are rated Master 3 specialists by the end of their first tour of duty.

Rudimentary school instruction and limited time and facilities for intensive shipboard on-the-job training and testing leaves the Soviet specialist able to perform only the more routine functions of maintenance and general operation of a very limited range of equipment. To alleviate some of these shortcomings shipboard equipment is, for the most part, assembled from standard components and modules.

Training At Sea

On board training is viewed as the major method of "perfecting skills and knowledge" to maintain a high level of combat readiness. Training at sea revolves around communist competition which entails the achievement of specified goals and objectives set by the commanding officer and political officer in conjunction with the staff. Some objectives and goals are prescribed in terms of the number of men achieving a new or higher class specialization and the number of men rated as outstanding.

Competitive drills and exercises are conducted aboard ship. These involve the usual variety of situations from damage control to simulated or actual firing of weapons. Fleet and inter-fleet exercises involve units competing against each other. All competition is characterized by the great emphasis that is placed upon obtaining set quantitative goals. This has resulted in a number of abuses. Aside from outright cheating, other abuses involve the setting of unrealistically low goals which are easily achieved, or the more serious problem of "formalism" in which, after the goals are set, promises made to fulfill them, all the required speeches made, then the whole competition is just forgotten. A further problem involves drills and exercises which are conducted in a routine, mechanical manner, thereby lacking realism and constructive value.

Obviously, the true extent to which these problems exist in Soviet training cannot be determined. Yet, if the reports of the Soviet press can be considered an indication, it would appear that such problems are not rare in Soviet training.

Shipboard Life

On his first tour of service the Soviet draftee receives low pay, even by Soviet standards (3.8 rubles per month—4.8 if on sea duty—which at the official exchange rate equals $6.50/mo.), and leave totaling only up to 20 days over a three year period. During this term of service he is under close supervision and

Figure 7

HIGHER NAVAL SCHOOLS (5-YEAR PROGRAMS)

School	Location	Specialization
Frunze Higher Naval School	Leningrad	Line
Makarov Pacific Ocean Higher Naval School	Vladivostok	Line
Kirov Red Banner Caspian Sea Higher Naval School	Baku	Line
Kaliningrad Higher Naval School	Kaliningrad	Line
Nakhimov Black Sea Higher Naval School	Sevastopol	Line
Leninskiy Komsomol Higher Naval School of Submarine Navigation	Leningrad	Submarine-line
Dzerahinskiy Order of Lenin Higher Naval Engineering School	Leningrad	Line-engineering
Sevastopol Higher Naval Engineering School	Sevastopol	Line-engineering
Popov Higher Naval Communications School	Leningrad Petrodvorets	Radio-electronics
Lenin Higher Naval Engineering School	Pushkin	Shore engineering
Kiev Higher Naval Political School	Kiev	Politics

POSTGRADUATE COURSES

Order of Lenin and Ushakov Naval Academy Imeni Marshal of the Soviet Union A. A. Grechko	Leningrad	Advanced technical and staff education (equivalent to U.S. Naval War College)
Naval Officers Technical School	Kronshtadt	Officer technical training
Higher Naval Courses	Leningrad	Officer technical training
Higher Military Academy of the General Staff (All Services)	Moscow	General staff training

subject to continuous political indoctrination. Sea duty can best be described as rigorous. Distant deployments often include long periods in open-water anchorages, and the infrequent liberty runs ashore in foreign ports are normally done in supervised groups during daylight hours. Living conditions aboard the modern classes of Soviet ships is, by Western standards, spartan but acceptable, whereas conditions aboard older classes, such as the PETYA and KOTLIN, are cramped and rather trying. Viewed in the relative terms of the standard of civilian housing in which many naval recruits previously lived, their shipboard accommodations are probably more than adequate.

C. Warrant Officers

The Soviet Navy faces a chronic shortage of senior enlisted personnel. The reenlistment rate averages under 10 percent, in part because of the national requirement that all males must serve on active duty in the Soviet armed forces. In an effort to overcome the aforementioned shortage, and to upgrade the status of a career serviceman the rank of warrant officer (Michman) was instituted in 1971. At completion of compulsory service the Soviet sailor, if considered capable, is offered additional specialist and military training in a two-year warrant officer school in return for a five-year reenlistment, including schooling.

Figure 8
COMPARISON OF SOVIET AND U.S. NAVAL GRADES AND RANKS
OFFICER GRADES

Rank*	Approximate U.S. Equivalent
Admiral of the Fleet of the Soviet Union	Fleet Admiral
Admiral of the Fleet	Admiral
Admiral	Vice Admiral
Vice Admiral	Rear Admiral
Rear Admiral	Commodore Admiral
Captain 1st Rank	Captain
Captain 2nd Rank	Commander
Captain 3rd Rank	Lieutenant Commander
Captain Lieutenant	Lieutenant
Senior Lieutenant	Lieutenant (junior grade)
Lieutenant	Ensign
Junior Lieutenant	Ensign

WARRANT GRADES

Warrant Officer (Michman)	Chief Warrant Officer
	Warrant Officer

NON-COMMISSIONED RANKS

Chief Ship's Petty Officer	Master Chief Petty Officer
	Senior Chief Petty Officer
Chief Petty Officer	Chief Petty Officer
Petty Officer First Class	Petty Officer First Class
Petty Officer Second Class	Petty Officer Second Class
Petty Officer Third Class	Petty Officer Third Class
Senior Seaman	Seaman
Seaman	Seaman Appretice/Recruit

*Naval aviation, naval infantry, and coastal defense personnel, although an integral part of the Navy, have "military" ranks, such as general, major, and sergeant.

Two Soviet sailors enjoy a "taste" of capitalism with a "hamburg and fries" during the Soviet Navy visit to Boston in commemoration of "VE" (Victory in Europe) day.

The warrant officer is designated the principal interface between officers and enlisted men. In this capacity he is given more responsibilities than a senior petty officer and, as a result of his more extensive training and experience, he can relieve the officers of some of the more technical duties which the conscript is not qualified to perform. Benefits increase considerably as pay, privileges, and leave offered to the warrant officer approach that of an officer. In addition, he is also offered the opportunity to achieve promotion to officer ranks after a number of years of service.

D. Officers

The regular sea-going Soviet naval officer, a career man, is a volunteer who has been carefully selected, well trained, and highly specialized. He is more often than not a relative of a Party official or another naval officer and ethnically, a Great Russian.

Schooling

The large majority of regular naval officers are now drawn from specialized naval schools. A small number begin as reserves after graduation from civilian universities and a few others win promotion from the warrant officer ranks. A youth normally starts his career as a cadet at one of 11 higher naval schools after a vigorous selection program. The course of study is intense and lasts five years, with the graduates receiving a National Engineering Diploma and the rank of lieutenant. Some Soviet officers begin their naval careers at about age 15 upon entering the Nakhimov naval school system for young men, and then going into a higher naval educational institution upon graduation from the Nakhimov school.

The higher naval schools can be divided into two types: line and engineering. Six line schools graduate officers as specialists in one of three areas: navigation, weapons, and antisubmarine warfare, which correspond to three of the five to seven departments of a Soviet warship. Graduates from one of three other higher naval engineering schools and one radio electronics school are assigned to ship radio electronics and engineering departments. There is also a higher naval school for shore duty engineering specialists and one which trains political officers for service with the fleet. Other naval specialist officers such as medical, legal, and finance are trained in higher schools with their army counterparts. Naval aviation officers receive their basic flight training with the Air Forces.

Early Career

Upon graduation, a regular officer is assigned to a ship for duty in the department which corresponds to his specialty (navigation, engineering, ASW, etc.). The new officer usually spends the first three to six years of his career in the same department aboard the same ship or at least in the same class of ship. During this period the new officer earns a classification as a specialist in his technical pursuit. He must pass the examinations to stand watch and for certification as a supervisor as he progresses through positions equivalent to assistant division officer, division officer, assistant department head, to department head.

Responsibilities

In the Soviet Navy the officer is both the manager of his unit and the major technical specialist. He is expected to be able to do virtually everything his subordinates can do, as well as to instruct them in their duties, and to care for their "ideological well being." Because of the general low level of technical competence of his enlisted men, the Soviet officer tends, in some cases, literally "to do everything," even the most routine maintenance. A Soviet junior officer's duties as manager, technician, instructor, and loyal Party member give him quite a heavy work load. Complaints are frequent, yet, in spite of these, the typical Soviet officer appears to fulfill his duties adequately.

Command

The selection of a commanding officer is a highly subjective process based on the principle that the commanding officer of a ship should select and train his own replacement. During the early years of an officer's service, his CO evaluates his performance and eligibility for command. As a vacancy occurs the ship's captain appoints the officer of his choice as executive officer and organizes and supervises a program of study for his development. During this period of study the line officer matures from a narrow specialist to a broad generalist capable of command. Upon successful completion of the demanding command-at-sea test, the officer succeeds the CO in command of the ship, or is assigned to command another ship of the same or a similar class. The length of time in an officer's first command varies with the individual and the ship, but averages between three to five years.

Those not considered qualified for command and those in the engineering categories, who, by virtue of their specialty, are not considered for command, become career specialists. Officers in these fields continue to receive promotions while serving as department heads and on staffs afloat or ashore.

E. Senior Officers

Considerable emphasis is placed on post-graduate education, and after command at sea an advanced

A Soviet rear admiral and his staff discuss mutual interests with a U.S. rear admiral during the visit of two Soviet destroyers to Boston. Soviet naval officers tend to be more specialized than their U.S. counterparts, with a major effort being undertaken to broaden their education as they approach selection for flag rank.

Soviet sailors, several with cameras, prepare to go ashore as their guided missile destroyer visits Massawa, Ethiopia. Although Soviet Navy life is spartan by American standards, modern Soviet warships are relatively comfortable and naval service provides these young men with travel and technical training opportunities not available to most of their countrymen.

degree is considered a prerequisite for posts of higher responsibility and flag rank. Officers with an average of six to eight years of experience, usually after their first command, take graduate training at the Grechko Naval Academy, an institution roughly equivalent to the U.S. Naval War College, or other schools offering advanced degrees. As an alternative to study in residence at a higher naval school, an officer can obtain an advanced degree by correspondence, requiring only limited residence.

After graduate work, the senior line officer generally serves on the staff of a group of ships of the same class that he commanded. Later, he rotates between fleets and other related tours are assigned to develop broader experience. Further, either immediately before or after promotion to flag rank, he will usually attend the joint service academy for general staff officers.

For those officers in "career specialties" the logical assignment after graduate training is to a position on the faculty of one of the naval schools or to a tour in one of the technical directorates (such as shipbuilding, mines, or torpedoes), as he proceeds toward flag-rank position in his area of expertise.

From the brief discussion above several major deficiencies may be clearly discerned in the education and experience of the Soviet naval officer. He spends the first part of his career as a specialist in a very narrow field, restricted to one department in one class of ship. As a result, the junior officer lacks needed broad experience and versatility. Often it is only upon selection as executive officer that he begins to develop the broader experience necessary for more senior posts. Because of the strong emphasis on collective thinking and Party-enforced discipline, the junior officer is often seriously lacking in personal initiative, original thinking, and the willingness to take responsibility; leadership characteristics that are necessary for command. But for those chosen to move up the promotion ladder, the positions held, education received, and training taken from mid-career onward imply that an officer finally selected

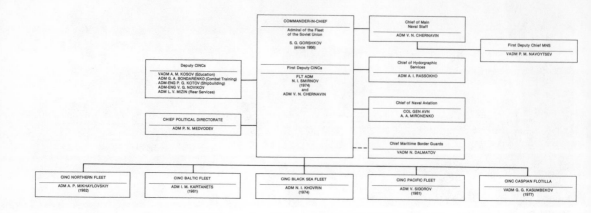

Figure 9
SOVIET NAVY HIGH COMMAND

for flag rank is both educated and experienced.

The base pay for Soviet officers initially appears nominal, but taken in combination with the total allowances and benefits which accrue to a military officer in the Soviet Union, the real income is substantial. For example, naval officers are given significant additional pay for service in northern areas, for service in submarines and aircraft, for sea duty, and for command. Military officers are a prestigious and privileged class in the Soviet Union and receive extensive benefits, according to rank, well beyond those of the average citizen.

F. Leadership

The highest office in the Soviet Navy is that of Commander-in-Chief (CINC). The position, currently held by Admiral of the Fleet of the Soviet Union Sergei G. Gorshkov, carries with it responsibilities for the operation and administration of the Soviet Navy. In addition, as head of one of the five military services, he serves as a Deputy Minister of Defense, a political position, which in the United States is filled by the Secretary of the Navy. Thus, Gorshkov simultaneously holds positions which in the U.S. would be equal to Chief of Naval Operations and Secretary of the Navy. Directly below the CINC is the First Deputy Commander-in-Chief, Admiral of the Fleet N.I. Smirnov, who is the assistant to the CINC in the operational direction of the fleet.

At the next level are five Deputy CINCs responsible for several different administrative, technical, logistical, and training functions. Additionally, there is a Navy Staff composed of the heads of several directorates which serves the CINC in policy and planning. Below this level are the fleet commanders. Each fleet is headed by a flag officer, with the fleet organizational structure quite similar to that of the CINC of the Soviet Navy.

Soviet flag officers tend to remain in their posts longer than their U.S. counterparts, with Admiral Gorshkov being the exceptional case in point. He has been CINC of the Soviet Navy since January of 1956! There have been several recent changes in senior naval posts and rumors persist that Gorshkov, born in 1910, will step down shortly. The most likely candidates to succeed him are Admiral Chernavin, Chief of the Main Naval Staff since 1982 and before that commander of the important Northern Fleet, and Fleet Admiral Smirnov, the first deputy CINC since 1974.

First deputy CINC since 1974 Admiral Chernavin has recently been designated as a First Deputy CINC while still serving as chief of MNS.

Admirals in senior positions are generally in their late fifties and early sixties. A signficant aspect of the Soviet philosophy toward high-level positions is that long term assignments and specialization do not necessarily destroy flexibility or effectiveness in leadership.

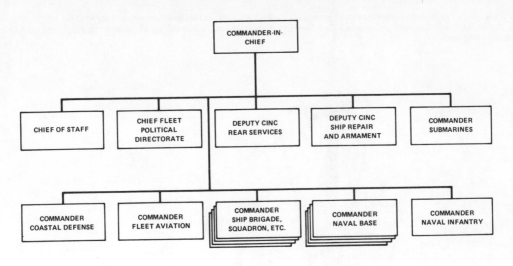

Figure 10

FLEET ORGANIZATION

G. Political Activity

All sectors of the Soviet military are subject to political indoctrination and close Communist Party monitoring which is even more extensive than in the civilian sector. Of course, a higher percentage of Soviet naval officers are Party members than in the civilian population. The stress upon political reliability is all-encompassing and of foremost importance. This stems from the concern of the Party to maintain a military force that is completely subordinate, thereby rendering it incapable of exercising military power for its own political ends.

Americans generally have difficulty differentiating between the Soviet State and the Communist Party, and hence the relationship of the Navy to the Party. The difficulty is, that for all intents and purposes, the State and the Party are indivisible. Their key leaders are virtually the same and their goals are identical. In essence, the Politburo of the Central Committee of the Communist Party is the ruling body of the U.S.S.R. with the "state" organization primarily running the day-to-day business of the nation. Several members of the Politburo also serve on the Presidium of the Supreme Soviet (or Congress), with the Presidium being the highest state body.

Over 90 percent of all naval officers are members of the Party or the Komsomol (Young Communist League). It is a rare officer who has not learned that demonstrating one's political activity is essential to a successful career. Further, Party membership is essential to obtain command. The Party, with representatives at all echelons of command within the armed forces, is headed in the Navy by a four-star admiral. Each ship has a political officer (Zampolit) who has his own separate chain of command. His duties aboard ship are diverse: he directs the ideological indoctrination and monitors the political reliability of the officers and men; directs "socialist" competition; ensures that Party decisions are carried out; enforces discipline; and acts as both "chaplain" and social worker for the crew to promote morale.

The nature of Party control sets up groups within the command structure; the CO and line officers comprise one part, and the political officer and the party organizations the other. Problems and tension are sometimes created between groups as they perform their functions. On one hand, an officer's military authority can be undermined since, as a member of the Party, he is as susceptible to party criticism and discipline as any other Party member. On the other hand, the Zampolit, while wearing the uniform of a naval officer, was in the past clearly not nautically qualified and, in many cases, was looked down upon by the professional naval officers. In recent years, however, there has been a trend toward giving the political officer practical naval experience as a line officer prior to his entry into the political field.

There is a significant commonality of interest between the Zampolit and the professional officers since both share responsibility for the successful operations of a ship and its performance in the "socialist" competition by which their careers are judged.

59

The Soviet thrust to the sea extends beyond warships. This photograph shows the passenger liner RUSSIA and a commercial hydrofoil at the Black Sea port of Odessa. The Soviet Union operates more passenger ships and more commercial hydrofoils than any other nation.

РОССИЯ

Section 6. Other Soviet Maritime Activities

". . .Among the main components which we included in the concept of the sea power of the state are the state's capabilities to study (investigate) the ocean and exploit its resources, the condition of the transport and fishing fleet and its ability to support the needs of the state, and also the presence of a navy adapted to the interests of that state, since antagonistic social systems are present in the world. . ."

Admiral of the Fleet of the Soviet Union
S.G. GORSHKOV

The extensive and intensive use of the sea by the Soviet Union over the last two decades has not been limited to naval operations. In the best traditions of Mahan, the Soviets have embraced the whole spectrum of activities which are considered part of the Sea Power "equation"—merchant marine, fishing, oceanographic research, shipbuilding, a large pool of experienced seamen, and a knowledgeable leadership.

The Soviet concept of sea power encompasses constant and coordinated use of all aspects of its natural, scientific, industrial, merchant, and naval resources in support of state policy. All the various elements of Soviet maritime activity have been developed by the deliberate allocation of resources as a matter of prime importance to the Soviet Union.

A. Merchant Marine

The application of the Soviet basic philosophy of sea power is clearly demonstrated in the ongoing development of the Merchant Marine. At the end of World War II the Soviet oceangoing merchant fleet consisted of about 400 ships totaling approximately two million deadweight tons. The ships were relatively small, old, and slow. In fact, the newest and best were the lend-lease "Liberty" ships that the United State had provided the Soviets during World War II.

In just over three decades, the Soviet oceangoing merchant fleet has emerged from an insignificant, coastal oriented flotilla to rank fifth in the world in numbers of ships, and ninth in terms of deadweight (carrying) tonnage. The expansion continues. Today the Soviet Union has an oceangoing merchant fleet of over 1,720 ships aggregating over 19 million deadweight tons. By comparison, the U.S. Mer-

chant Marine, with just over 560 ships equalling approximately 21 million deadweight tons, ranks tenth in number of ships and seventh in carrying capacity. However, the U.S. Merchant fleet is largely composed of large tankers and non-self-sustaining container ships, units which would be less advantageous to us in time of crisis.

The Soviet merchant fleet is presently operating on over 70 different international trade routes, calling at over 125 countries throughout the world. Prior to the boycott by U.S. longshoremen, a result of the Afghan invasion, Soviet merchant ships were calling at nearly 60 different ports along the U.S. East, West, and Gulf coasts as well as in the Great Lakes.

The growth of the Soviet Merchant Marine has paralleled a period of equally dramatic world-wide maritime development, but the Soviet accomplishments have been unique. While the international growth has been spurred by the demand for big oil tankers, bulk carriers and container ships, the Soviet Union has carefully directed the growth of its merchant fleet, not allowing purely commercial pressures of modern trade to dictate its composition. It is of interest to note that while most nations have reduced their passenger-carrying fleets, the Soviets continue to expand theirs and today have the largest passenger fleet in the world.

As a result, the Soviets today possess one of the few major merchant fleets which can perform either a peacetime commercial mission or satisfy military logistics requirements effectively and efficiently should a conflict arise. This has been achieved by accepting some economic disadvantages in exchange for functional versatility. Rather than building only supertankers, container ships, liquid gas tankers and bulk carriers, the Soviets have improved the designs of their large, sophisticated cargo ships and small, multi-purpose tankers. They also have stressed the building of high-speed, Roll-On/Roll-Off (RO/RO) combination vehicle and container ships. The RO/RO ships offer the Soviets considerable versatility.

The RO/RO ship is basically a floating garage that loads and unloads cargo via a large ramp, so it can easily transport most forms of military hardware without ship modification. Moreover, it does not need sophisticated port facilities. The Soviet Union has more than 40 RO/RO ships operational and other numerous specialized ships are scheduled to be delivered in the near future. These ships can operate on the most competitive commercial routes, yet they can be, and have been, reallocated with very little delay to serve as military sealift or logistics ships.

The Soviets have recently received two large, SEABEE barge transport ships (U.S. design) from Finland. The SEABEE represents another advanced concept in cargo handling; it can transport large unit loads, such as 1,300-ton barges, and has the potential for use in military logistics or amphibious lift operations. Cargo is loaded with a stern-mounted, 2,700-ton-capacity elevator. Up to 25,000 tons of cargo can be off-loaded in only 13 hours. A SEABEE ship could contribute significantly to Soviet military operations.

The Soviet 1976–1980 five-year plan calls for a growth in foreign trade of 30 to 35 percent, with particular emphasis on expansion of commerce with the capitalist world. In addition, the Soviet Union intends to use its merchant fleet to carry its own trade. Available figures indicate that the Soviet Merchant Marine transports approximately 60 percent of its own imports. (By comparison, the U.S. Merchant Marine carries less than five percent.)

The five-year plan also projects a cargo carrying capacity increase of over 4 million deadweight tons. If the net gain stated in their goal is reached, the Soviet oceangoing merchant fleet will consist of approximately 1,800 ships totaling nearly 19.5 million deadweight tons by 1981. All indications are that the following five-year plan will also see a 4 million deadweight ton growth.

The Soviet Merchant Marine has proved to be an effective tool for the extension of Soviet influence, as well as an instrument for neutralizing or eliminating free world influence in strategic areas. Past activities of the merchant fleet in support of Soviet State policy, especially in African, Middle Eastern, and Indian Ocean waters, are contributing to a growing political acceptance of the Soviet presence in these areas.

The Merchant Marine, on a regular basis, provides a significant amount of the logistics support required by the Soviet Navy, particularly to those ships operating in waters distant from the U.S.S.R. This gives the Soviet Navy a high degree of flexibility in the employment of its forces. Additionally, these merchant ships have a much greater freedom of access to the ports of the world than do navy ships or auxiliaries and thus can purchase fresh water, produce and other supplies for naval use in

A Soviet roll-on/roll-off (RO/RO) ship lowers her 60-ton capacity stern ramp to take aboard vehicles.

ports where warship visits might be denied.

Today, Soviet merchant ships operate on all oceans, calling at ports throughout the globe. If a Soviet ship is in distress in distant waters, it usually is only a matter of hours before other Soviet ships arrive at the scene to assist.

In summary, Soviet leaders, no doubt, see the Merchant Marine providing the following advantages and capabilities:

- a large national resource providing valuable hard-currency income, services, and employment;
- an instrument to provide support for the foreign policy of the state and to further the cause of Soviet Communism;
- a source of much needed foreign currency in a continuing "balance of payments" battle;
- a visible sign to the world of the prestige and power of the Soviet Union;
- a training system for an expanding pool of trained seamen;
- a closely coordinated logistics force for meeting the needs of the Soviet Navy on a regular basis.
- a world-wide network of intelligence collection; and
- a highly organized, closely controlled organization which can provide military support quickly and effectively, particularly for amphibious operations or arms movements.

Overall, the Soviet Union is expected to continue to develop a multi-mission Merchant Marine which can compete economically in international markets and provide many other services in support of State policy, while maintaining the ability to respond rapidly to any need for extensive military support. Thus, the merchant fleet provides the U.S.S.R. with a growing capability for the world-wide support of political, military, and economic influence.

B. Fishing

The Soviet Union operates the world's largest fishing fleet with nearly 4,000 ocean-going vessels. The fleet's catch in 1975 exceeded 10 million tons. This catch placed the Soviets second behind Japan, and was more than three times the size of the U.S. catch.

Considerable resources have been invested in the fishing industry in the postwar period, with emphasis on the construction of large, high-capacity ocean-going ships equipped with elaborate fish-finding devices and processing facilities.

The Soviets exploit fishing grounds throughout the world's oceans with large flotillas of ships. Groups of 100 to 200 trawlers are not unusual and, on occasion, much larger formations have been reported. Trawlers which can handle up to 50 tons of fish per day often are equipped to filet, salt, can or freeze the catch on board. Large factory ships and refrigerated cargo ships also receive processed and unprocessed fish from the smaller trawlers. The factory ships have the necessary processing and

The sleek-looking passenger liner MAKSIM GORKIY at a Far Eastern port. The Soviets use many of their passenger ships in the lucrative vacation cruise trade to earn hard Western currency. The Soviets have approximately 70 large passenger ships in service.

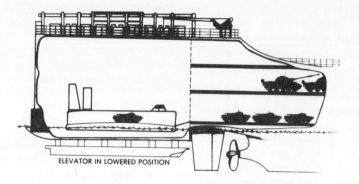

ELEVATOR IN LOWERED POSITION

storage facilities aboard and can transfer their fish products at sea to cargo ships which take them to market. There is little waste—that part of the catch which is not processed into food is usually turned into fish meal or fertilizer without delay.

These fishing flotillas are usually self-contained "communities," supported by specialized repair ships, tugs, tankers, and fresh water vessels. On occasion these auxiliary ships also support naval activities. When a Soviet HOTEL class ballistic missile

This port-quarter stern view of the Soviet merchant ship INZEHENER MACHULSKIY shows the ship's stern ramp in the raised position. She is a roll-on/roll-off vehicle-carrying ship with space for coontainers or vehicles on her main deck. The Soviet merchant marine is large, modern, and flexible.

submarine encountered engineering difficulties in the North Atlantic in 1972 the submarine was assisted for several days by support ships for the fishing fleet.

Soviet fishermen are among the highest paid workers in the U.S.S.R. They are compensated for the hardships of long voyages and climatic extremes with annual paid vacations often exceeding two months. The industry also is a major employer of Soviet naval reservists.

Most fish caught by the Soviet Union (over 90 percent) is for human consumption and eaten by the Soviet people or given as aid to Soviet client states. It has been estimated that 20 percent of the Soviet protein consumption consists of seafood. Exports include such delicacies as caviar, squid, and king crab. The latter is caught in great quantities off the coast of Alaska, and has been the subject of a continuing controversy as well as given rise to several treaties between the United States and the Soviet Union.

The Soviet's large whaling fleet has also brought it (and that of the Japanese) into a running conflict with world conservationists who are seeking to save a number of whale species from extinction.

Since the Soviet fishing flotillas "invaded" U.S. coastal fishing grounds in 1961, there has been much debate on Soviet "vacuum cleaner" fishing methods and the damage done to the U.S. fishing industry. The establishment in 1977 of a 200-mile economic zone around the United States has placed limits on catch and strict control of fishing activities on foreign fishing ships within the zone. Masters of several Soviet fishing vessels have been placed under arrest by the U.S. Coast Guard for violating these controls. The Soviets are now faced with a large number of such economic zones established by countries with contiguous traditional fishing grounds.

The "universality" of fishing has led to considerable export of Soviet fishing equipment and technology to other countries. Similarly the Soviet Union has purchased a large number of fishing units from East German, Poland, and other nations.

The Soviet merchant ship BALASHIKHA is pushed to a pier by harbor tugs at Nantes, France. In addition to servicing the long Soviet coastlines, the Soviet merchant fleet carries on an active and profitable trade with the West and the Third World.

The massive Soviet fishing fleet has its own training and research ships, the latter including the EKVATOR shown here. For several years two converted WHISKEY-class submarines were employed in the fisheries/oceanographic research role. They have been discarded.

It is likely that there will be a continuing growth in the quality of the fishing industry and in the size of its fishing fleet as well. There are indications that in the not too distant future, the Soviets will be the undisputed world leader in this area of maritime endeavor, which is increasing in importance as the earth's population grows and seeks additional animal protein.

C. Research and Surveying

Soviet maritime activity is supported by the world's largest fleet of ocean-going research and surveying ships, totaling over 200 ships. These ships are separate from the naval intelligence ships (AGI) discussed in Section 4. Rather, they are engaged in academic and economic studies and operational research of the oceans. A number of these ships are Navy subordinated and manned by Navy crews, but the majority belongs to civilian institutes concerned with ocean research and are civilian manned. Obviously, the civilian segments of research activities have close ties with those of the Soviet Navy and, again, the officers of the civilian manned ships include a number of naval reservists. In addition, the

A Soviet "fish factory" ship operates with part of her brood of smaller fishing craft off Cape Cod in the Western Atlantic. These large ships are floating bases and can completely process and can a catch on board. The Soviet Union has more than 4,000 ocean-going fishing craft and support ships, plus numerous inshore fishing boats, all directed by a centralized ministry.

The Soviet satellite tracking ship KOSMONAUT YURI GAGARIN is one of a fleet of Soviet Space Events Support Ships (SESS) which are employed in civilian and military space and missile programs. The large, sophisticated ships of this type have secondary intelligence collection and political presence capabilities. Most of these ships are operated by civilian research institutes, with a few others being Navy manned.

Soviet Union operates a large number of Space Event Support Ships (designated SESS) that provide worldwide spacecraft and satellite tracking and recovery capabilities. This extensive use of SESS units is in marked contrast with the U.S. policy of primarily placing space tracking stations ashore around the world.

Activities of the research, surveying, and space support ships are managed by the several institutes of the Academy of Sciences of the U.S.S.R. that direct scientific research. These institutes maintain close coordination with both the Navy and the Main Fisheries Administration, with the latter organization operating several research ships. During the 1960s two modified Navy submarines also were used for fishing research and in the 1970s several naval submarines were employed on oceanographic research expeditions.

Soviet research ships are generally of modern design with most being of Finnish, Polish or East German construction. These ships vary in size from small coastal craft to the giant KOSMONAUT YURI GAGARIN, a 45,000 ton ship fitted with elaborate equipment for research into the upper atmosphere and support of space events.

D. Shipbuilding

The current Soviet shipbuilding industry evolved after World War II when the devastated yards of the Baltic and Black Sea coasts were rebuilt. Additionally, new yards were constructed (or enlarged) on the Northern and Pacific coasts to make those naval fleets more independent of the traditional European yards.

Today the Soviet Union has 19 large shipyards, each employing 2,000 or more workers on a fulltime basis. It is not, therefore, unreasonable to state that the U.S.S.R. ranks as one of the world's largest producers of ships. However, because of the Soviet emphasis on small merchant ships and fishing craft, the Soviet tonnage production is small for the number of ships produced.

Besides receiving the output of a large indigenous ship-building industry, the Soviets also purchase a considerable amount of merchant and naval tonnage from foreign yards. Naval ships, particularly amphibious ships and auxiliaries are purchased from Poland, Finland, and East German as are merchant and fishing ships from the aforementioned countries plus others, including France, Japan, West Germany, Sweden, and Great Britain.

Soviet submarines are built at Severodvinsk on the White Sea, the largest submarine building complex in the world; at Komsomolsk, well up the Amur River near the Pacific coast; at Gorkiy, which is in the center of the U.S.S.R., with ships moving to the open sea via the extensive Soviet inland waterway system; and, at the two-yard United Admiralty complex in Leningrad. It is estimated that these yards have capacities great enough to produce 20 to 25 nuclear submarines a year on a single-shift basis, if priority was given to allocating necessary resources and labor from other sources. The Soviets have been building about 8 or 9 new submarines annually, most nuclear powered, over the last several years.

Principal surface combatants are, for the most part, built in Leningrad and Kaliningrad on the Baltic Sea, and Nikolayev near the Black Sea where the KIEV class carriers were constructed. A number of other yards are involved in the construction of lesser combatants and other types of naval ships.

Most of the shipyards which build warships also build merchant or fishing ships. The construction of all ships, naval or commercial, in the Soviet Union is managed by the Ministry of Shipbuilding. This ministry is responsible for all yards of significant size; for most research, design, and useful exchange of technologies; and for a coordinated allocation of resources. Each aspect of ship design, construction, and specialized equipment is supported by a specialized research institute.

New shipbuilding equipment, from a simple hand tool to a computer-controlled cutting machine, must be approved by the Ministry of Shipbuilding before it is introduced as a standard item. Similarly, techniques initially employed for merchant construction (such as modular assembly of components on a floating platform) subsequently are applied to naval shipbuilding.

The KOSMONAUT VLADIMIR KOMAROV is also a Soviet Space Events Support Ship (SESS) named in honor of a deceased astronaut. The ship's radar antennas are enclosed in plastic spheres; the horn-like antennas on the masts are for satellite communications.

The oceanographic research ship AKADEMIK SASHKIRIYA, shown here underway in the South China Sea, is a modern AGOR built in East Germany for Soviet service. The civilian-manned ship is typical of the large Soviet ocean research fleet that supports military and civil activities.

The Soviet yards make extensive use of modern shipbuilding techniques and technologies. According to a U.S. Navy report on the subject: "In formulating a judgment on U.S.S.R. progress in automation of (ship) production . . . most of the publicized innovations are related to yards doing merchant work of a far more open nature and considerably lower priority than Soviet naval work, and it can therefore be presumed that in yards engaged in high priority work on naval ships, the facilities, equipment, and technology are at least equal and probably superior. . ." Various Soviet shipbuilding management and production techniques that have been observed have led to the conclusion that the Soviets have established a very strong and viable shipbuilding industry.

In addition to building naval and commercial ships for Soviet use, Soviet shipyards have produced ships of both categories for other nations in the Warsaw Pact, Western Europe, and the Third World.

Section 7. Key Questions

1. Which Navy is the larger?

In terms of the ships the U.S. Navy is clearly outnumbered by the Soviet Navy, by a ratio of 3 to 1. Although we dominate in aircraft carriers, the Soviet Navy has 80 more principal surface combatants, 250 more submarines, six times as many auxiliaries, and a large land-based aviation strike force. Amphibious ships of the U.S. Navy are much larger and more capable, but this is a warfare area where the Soviets have greatly increased their capability over the last decade. Furthermore, the quality of their naval forces is steadily improving, though it is still not equal to the quality of our own. The U.S. Navy clearly has a large advantage in sea-based aircraft and a greater number of uniformed personnel.

In contrast to Soviet Navy forces, those of the U.S. Navy have declined substantially since the late 1960's. These reductions have restricted our flexibility in fulfilling peacetime commitments worldwide, and limited our offensive options in many critical and high threat areas in time of war. A strategy of sequential offensive campaigns based on a careful alignment of our objectives in order of relative importance is required for the U.S. to succeed in gaining effective control of those sea areas essential to our successful prosecution of a global war.

The table overleaf depicts the trends in the size of U.S. and U.S.S.R. naval forces, and illustrates the marked decline in the size of the U.S. Navy since 1969. By comparison, Soviet reductions have been modest and primarily involve the retirement of smaller coastal defense ships.

2. Which Navy is the stronger?

Simple numerical comparisons are but one measure for drawing conclusions about the strengths of navies. In the nuclear-electronic-missile age the "equation" has become most complicated. Also,

the U.S. and Soviet Navies have been built differently for different missions. The power potential of each, but more particularly the Soviet Navy, is related to the distance its naval forces operate from its homeland. Thus, the Soviets can bring much more weight of arms to bear close to the Soviet littoral than they can in mid-Atlantic or mid-Pacific. In some functions the Soviet Navy is the stronger, while in others the U.S. Navy excels.

The U.S. Navy is generally considered to lead in the areas of:

> Carrier Aviation
> Amphibious Assault
> Submarine Detection
> Submarine Noise Level Control
> Underway Replenishment
> Nuclear Surface Ships

The Soviet Navy is generally considered to lead in:

> Antiship Missiles
> Number of Submarines
> Small Combat Craft
> Ocean Surveillance
> New Technology Application
> Shipbuilding Capacity and Initiative
> Mine Warfare
> Integration of Maritime Resources
> Numbers of Conventional Surface Ships
> Command and Control Structure

With respect to a comparison of U.S. and Soviet Navies, Admiral Gorshkov has observed that:

The qualitative transformations which have taken place in naval forces have also changed the approach to evaluating the relative might of navies and their combat groupings: we have had to cease comparing the number of warships of one type or another and their

A Soviet ALFA-class nuclear-powered submarine—the world's fastest and deepest diving combat undersea craft.

71

total displacement (or the number of guns in a salvo or the weight of this salvo), and turn to a more complex but also more correct appraisal of the striking and defensive power of ships, based on a mathematical analysis of their capabilities and qualitative characteristics.

3. Should NATO navies be countered in U.S.-Soviet comparisons?

Most definitely, and the navies of the Soviet's Warsaw Pact allies should also be counted in these types of net comparisons. If the U.S. and the Soviet Navy should ever go to war it would most likely be a NATO/Warsaw Pact conflict. The contributions of the NATO navies to the Alliance are considerable.

Strategically, Britain and France each operate a small force of nuclear powered ballistic missile submarines. Britain, Canada and France have significant naval forces and maritime commitments beyond European waters. Yet most NATO naval forces are designed to operate in the littoral waters of Europe supporting NATO's flanks and keeping the vital sea lanes open. Therefore, other NATO navies concentrate in coastal defense, antisubmarine and mine warfare tasks, with NATO assignments, for the most part, in waters proximate to their homelands. U.S. naval forces seldom operate in the Baltic and Black Seas where the great bulk of maritime defense rests on the NATO countries whose shores are washed by those seas.

It must be remembered, however, that the second most powerful force in the Soviet Navy is the Pacific Ocean Fleet which, except for its naval air element, is too far removed from the NATO area of responsibility to be an immediate threat. But that fleet is of prime concern to the U.S. and our Pacific allies, for one must accept that a NATO/Warsaw Pact war could not be confined to the European area. Therefore, the Soviet Pacific threat can not be divorced from that in Europe.

4. Why have the Soviets waited so long to build aircraft carriers?

Since the dramatic changes in Soviet government and policies of the mid-1950s the Soviet Navy has not always attempted to compete where the U.S. Navy is strongest. Rather, the Soviets have developed other forces and weapons to counter the U.S. Navy, such as submarines and antiship missiles. Initially it would have been very difficult for them to compete in an areas of naval warfare such as carrier aviation with the same type of assets. The United States already had several decades of experi-

Figure II.
NAVAL COMBATANT FORCE LEVEL TRENDS

		1969 US /USSR		1983 US /USSR	
ACTIVE	**FLEET**				
Submarines		156	354	135	375
Aircraft Carriers		22	0	13	3
Helicopter Carriers		8	2	12	2
Surface Combatants		279	218	188	279
Command Ships		2	0	2	0
Missile/Large Patrol Types		9	148	6	150
Amphibious Warfare Ships		145	103	51	85
Mine Countermeasure Ships		74	165	3	145
Mobile Logistic Ships		112	56	53	80
Auxiliary Support Ships		119	624	35	700
TOTAL ACTIVE FLEET		926	1670	497	1819
NAVAL RESERVE FORCE					
Surface Combatants		35	**	5	**
Patrol Combatants		6	**	0	**
Amphibious Warfare Ships		1	**	2	**
Mine Countermeasure Ships		14	**	18	**
Mobile Logistic Ships		0	**	0	**
Auxiliary Support Ships		1	**	0	**
TOTAL NAVAL RESERVE FORCE		57		25	
NAVAL FLEET AUXILIARY FORCE (U.S. Civilian manned)					
Mobile Logistic Ships		0	***	17	***
Auxiliary Support Ships		4	***	7	***
TOTAL FLEET AUXILIARY FORCE		4		24	
TOTAL OPERATING FORCE		1007	**	547	1819 +

ence as well as an existing force of supercarriers along with their highly specialized aircraft.

Also significant is the fact that one of the prime missions of the U.S. Navy in time of war includes the projection of power overseas to support allies and protect broad ocean areas. The aircraft carrier is a key factor in the "projection" and "sea control" missions. Soviet "projection" forces to date have been primarily either politico-economic in concept, ground military forces, or naval surface ships. Other priorities had to be met in the Soviet order before the large endeavor of aircraft development could be undertaken.

Construction of the KIEV class carriers, however, now demonstrates that the time has arrived for aircraft carrier-type ships to be added to the Soviet Navy. Along with the Soviet development of amphibious forces, the Soviet Navy will greatly improve its ability to meet sea control and projection objectives with the addition of the KIEVs, the expected larger carrier of the eighties, the new warship classes under construction, and the expanding merchant marine. Some observers see the carrier and the aforementioned programs as the instruments with which the Soviets plan, for the first time, to challenge U.S. Naval supremacy on the high seas beyond the waters which the Soviets currently view as critical to their defense.

5. How experienced is the Soviet Navy?

The Soviet Navy had minimal open ocean combat experience in World War II and none since that war. By comparison, some senior officers of the U.S. Navy saw extensive combat during World War II, and others in the Navy as a whole have had considerable combat experience in certain combat disciplines during the Korean and Vietnam wars. Also, U.S. naval personnel have had considerably more ocean-going experience during the three decades since World War II. However, the Soviets are rapidly expanding their pool of trained seafarers in the Navy as well as in the merchant and fishing fleets. Their ability to operate ships and aircraft over the oceans of the world at great distances from the Soviet Union has increased steadily.

6. Are aircraft carriers vulnerable to Soviet Missiles?

Soviet air, surface, and submarine-launched guided or cruise missiles are the primary military threat to all surface warships. However, the aircraft carrier is probably the least vulnerable and most survivable because of its extensive damage-control features and the inherent defensive capabilities of its embarked air wing. The aircraft carrier is essentially a mobile airbase, giving it greater flexibility and subject to less political sensitivity than a fixed base. Also in certain other aspects a carrier is less vulnerable—it can maneuvered to minimize risk, is not subject to political denial, and is not susceptible to guerilla attack.

The modern U.S. aircraft carrier is thus considered highly survivable in comparison with other general purpose forces, and at the same time, is recognized (particularly by the Soviets) as one of the most powerful and versatile weapon systems ever developed.

The VICTOR III attack submarine, in series production, is a high-speed undersea craft with advanced antisubmarine weapons and acoustic detection gear, including a towed array fitted in the pod atop the rudder.

Appendix A. COMMENTS BY THE SECRETARY OF DEFENSE ON SOVIET NAVAL DEVELOPMENTS

The following comments on the development of the Soviet Navy are excerpted from SOVIET MILITARY POWER, *a report on Soviet military developments, signed by Secretary of Defense Caspar W. Weinberger in March 1983. The entire document is available from the Government Printing Office, Washington, D.C.*

STRATEGIC MISSILE SUBMARINES

Over the last two years the Soviets have continued to modernize their submarine launched ballistic missile (SLBM) force. A second TYPHOON-class nuclear-powered ballistic missile submarine (SSBN) has been launched at the Severodvinsk shipyard; the first TYPHOON completed its sea trials and has moved to port facilities on the north coast of the Kola Peninsula. Armed with 20 launchers for the MIRVed SS-NX-20 solid-fueled SLBM, the first submarine of this class will be fully operational by the end of 1983. The range of the SS-NX-20, 8,300 kilometers, places all of NATO Europe, North America and Asia within TYPHOON's reach.

While the TYPHOON SSBN production program is still relatively new, the Soviets' earlier DELTA III program is nearing completion. Thus far, 14 of these SSBNs have been launched; a few more will probably be built. Each carries 16 liquid-fueled MIRVed SS-N-18 SLBMs.

Like the TYPHOON, the missiles on the DELTA III, as well as the DELTA I and II, can reach targets in almost all of North America from home waters. By contrast, only the TRIDENT C-4 has similar range capabilities. However, the bulk of U.S. SLBMs is much less capable in terms of range, accuracy and yield.

With the addition of each new SSBN, the Soviet Navy has dismantled older submaries in order to remain within the number of launchers (950) and number of hulls (62) allowed under provisions of the SALT-I Agreement, as extended. The addition

to the force of some 200 reentry vehicles (RVs) on each TYPHOON, however, greatly eclipses the temporary reduction caused by the dismantlement of one YANKEE-class SSBN (48 RVs) and of two HOTEL II class SSBNs (total 6 RVs) in compensation for a newly constructed TYPHOON. The acquisition of each new SSBN equipped with SS-N-18/SS-NX-20 SLBMs not only introduces more RVs but also allows the Soviets greater flexibility in the use of their new submarines. Older SSBNs with shorter-ranged SLBMs have to conduct lengthy transits in order to come within range of targets in North America.

Future developments in Soviet SLBMs will most likely center on improved RV accuracy to complement their estimated large nuclear yields and on the fielding of solid-fueled SLBMs as replacements for older liquid-fueled versions. A new SLBM, possibly intended to replace the SS-N-18, probably will begin testing in 1983.

Apart from its SLBMs, the Soviet Navy will soon be the recipient of a sea-launched cruise missile (SLCM) that is currently under development, the SS-NX-21. With an estimated maximum range on the order of 3,000 kilometers, its mission is primarily nuclear strike, and its size is compatible with submarine torpedo tubes.

Theater Naval Forces

The Soviet Navy surface ships, submarines and aircraft arrayed against NATO are in the Northern Fleet, the Baltic Fleet and the Black Sea Fleet. Improvements in these forces during the course of the

e SVERDLOV class cruiser ALEKSANDR SUVORO, "with a bone in her teeth" steams in the Philippine Sea during the Exer-e OKEAN. Although some 30 years old, the Soviets still utilize these old "work horses" extensively.

past five years have encompassed all aspects of naval warfare and have involved numerous individual weapon systems. The principal missions of Soviet surface combatants, attack submarines and Soviet naval aviation include the protection of the seaborne approaches to the Soviet Union and Warsaw Pact Allies and the isolation of NATO forces from reinforcement and resupply.

In addition to submarines and major surface combatants, Soviet construction programs have produced minor combatants well suited to theater level combat operations. Since 1978, units of four new classes of ocean and coastal patrol craft have entered service, including guided-missile patrol combatants, missile-equipped hydrofoil patrol craft, torpedo-equipped patrol hydrofoils and antisubmarine warfare patrol combatants. In addition to providing modern platforms with significant offensive firepower to supplant or replace obsolescent units, all of these minor combatants demonstrate improved air defense capabilities.

A major responsibility of the Soviet Navy is support to Warsaw Pact ground forces to include defense of their maritime flanks and the conduct of amphibious warfare operations.

Soviet Naval Infantry units assigned to the Northern, Baltic, and Black Sea Fleets have undergone a major reorganization, resulting in an increase in organic firepower. These units have received self-propelled howitzers and additional multiple rocket launchers, antitank weapons and medium tanks.

The Pacific Ocean Fleet, the largest of the Soviet Navy's four fleets, has grown steadily since the mid-1960s from about 50 principal surface combatants to over 80 today. The 1979 assignment of the KIEV-class aircraft carrier MINSK to the Pacific Fleet highlights the qualitative aspects of the improvements that have taken place. The MINSK is equipped with FORGER VTOL attack aircraft and HORMONE antisubmarine warfare (ASW) helicopters. A second carrier of this class will likely join the Pacific Fleet during this decade. Three KARA-class guided missile ASW cruisers have also joined the fleet since 1978.

Equally impressive have been the improvements in the Soviet submarine force in the Pacific, which numbers over 30 ballistic missile submarines, and over 90 attack submarines—including substantial numbers of modern VICTOR III nuclear-powered attack submarines (SSN), CHARLIE I nuclear-powered cruise missile submarines (SSGN), and the new diesel-electric powered KILO conventional attack submarine. These submarines give the Pacific Fleet a substantially improved capability in antisubmarine and anticarrier warfare.

Soviet Naval Aviation has grown by over 50 percent since the mid-1960s to a current force of about 400 aircraft. The deployment of over 30 naval long-

A BORIS CHILIKEN class replenishment oiler refuels a KYNDA class missile cruiser underway with two span wires supporting five refueling hoses.

range BACKFIRE B aircraft to the Far East since 1980—in addition to the Air Force BACKFIREs in the region—has significantly increased the threat to shipping in large expanses of the Pacific.

The Pacific Fleet also includes the largest contingent of naval infantry in the Soviet Navy—an 8,000 man division based near Vladivostok. Elements of this elite, well-trained force deploy with naval forces in the Pacific and, on a limited scale, can rapidly respond to local contingencies.

The quality and quantity of Soviet forces in the Far East have been substantially improved, and these trends will continue in the future. The Soviets have a formidable capability to wage wars simultaneously in the West and East. Moreover, the Soviets have projected their military power in the Far East beyond their historic sphere of influence and have thereby enhanced their capability to challenge any nation or combination of nations in this region.

General Naval Forces

The missions of the Soviet Navy are two-fold: first, to protect the seaward approaches to Warsaw Pact territory and coastal waters including SSBN patrol areas and, second, to neutralize Allied maritime forces which could threaten the success of Soviet military operations. Each of these two major missions requires distinct groups of ships and aircraft. Generally, the forces protecting the sea approaches are larger in number, smaller in size, more oriented to a single task and less capable in terms of weapons and endurance. These forces are designed to gain and maintain control of waters contiguous to Warsaw Pact states and along the coastal flanks of ground force movements.

The second wartime mission results in an increasing trend toward sustained operations by large naval formations in all the world's major oceans. These forces comprise hundreds of strike bombers, attack submarines and surface warships. They are forces capable of firing eight types of medium and long-range nuclear-capable antiship cruise missiles and four types of missile-delivered long-range ASW weapons. These modern forces have been created as a result of improved design efforts and Soviet advances in nuclear and other technologies. Concurrently, the Soviets have constantly expanded their distant area operations to maintain a significant naval presence in the Mediterranean Sea, Indian Ocean, South China Sea and in the South Atlantic.

During the past several years, the Soviets have maintained a large naval construction program.

This vigorous program now comprises seven classes of surface warships, five classes of submarines and four aircraft types. Among the surface warship programs is the KIEV-class 38,000-ton VTOL aircraft carrier. In 1982, the third KIEV unit joined the fleet with the fourth unit expected to do so in 1984.

The second unit of the 28,000-ton KIROV-class cruiser—the first Soviet nuclear-powered surface warship—is nearing completion. This unit will have a significantly improved surface-to-air missile defense capability, and it is being fitted with a new SAM believed to be optimized to defend against sea-skimming cruise missiles. The first ship of the 12,500-ton gas-turbine-powered guided missile cruiser of the KRASINA-class has also entered service. This ship carries 16 antiship cruise missiles and an advanced vertical launch SAM system of the same type as that on the KIROV-class. Additional units of two classes of guided missile destroyers, the SOVREMENNYY (antisurface warfare) and the UDALOY (antisubmarine warfare), continue to augment the fleet.

Of the three nuclear and two diesel classes of attack submarines being produced, the most impressive is the 14,000-ton OSCAR-class carrying 24 SS-N-19 antiship cruise missiles with a range of 500 kilometers. This is more than three times as many cruise missiles than have been fitted on previous classes of series-produced Soviet submarines. Additionally the nuclear-powered, titanium-hulled ALFA-class torpedo attack submarines—at 40 knots the world's fastest—and the VICTOR III, fitted with the Soviets' first towed-array ASW sensor, are still entering the fleet at a rate of three per year. The TANGO and KILO-classes of diesel-powered attack submarines also continue to be constructed. The latter is currently being built and deployed only in the Far East, although deployments are expected to include the western fleets by 1984.

Among the aircraft still being built for Soviet Naval Aviation are the supersonic, variable-geometry wing BACKFIRE capable of carrying three 300-kilometer-range, Mach 3 air-to-surface antiship cruise missiles. The FORGER fighter-bomber also continues to be built to fill the air wings on the KIEV-class carrier. In late 1982, this aircraft, carrying air-to-air missiles, conducted a close-range interception of a U.S. Navy aircraft over the Indian Ocean.

In the near future, a new attack submarine will begin series production at two shipyards. This class will have significantly more capability than the older VICTOR III.

The Soviets soon will begin construction of a

large, nuclear-powered aircraft carrier that will carry conventional take-off and landing high-performance jet fighters. The first ship of this new class will probably enter naval service late in the decade. The Soviets will also continue to improve the combat capabilities of their antiship and antisubmarine weapons and sensors so that by the 1990s they will have greater capabilities to fight naval battles on the high seas far from home waters.

The following is the statement by the Director of Naval Intelligence, Rear Admiral John L. Butts, U.S. Navy, on the Soviet naval threat, presented to the Senate Armed Services Committee on 14 March 1983.

The death of Leonid Brezhnev [in November, 1982] has brought an 18-year chapter of Soviet history to an end. Its immediate legacy is a challenging array of foreign and domestic problems, including some military problems of the first order. The new leaders of the Soviet Union have their work cut out for them.

There were major changes in all branches of the Soviet military in those 18 years under Brezhnev. For the Soviet Navy, the changes were reflected in the way the Soviets are building their Navy and in the way in which they conduct naval operations.

Since 1964, the Soviets have built about 150 nuclear-powered submarines, 70 diesel submarines, 30 cruisers, 20 destroyers, 145 frigates, 75 amphibious landing ships and air cushion vehicles, and 140 naval auxiliaries and support ships, plus a considerable number of naval aircraft. They also have built four VTOL aircraft carriers; and they have expanded their naval infantry force from about 4,000 in 1964 to its present size of about 14,000 troops. The Soviet Navy now has enough modern ships and aircraft to provide a naval presence around the world and they are doing so on a day-to-day basis.

The Soviets launched new ships in 1982 at roughly the same pace as 1981, although in both years the number launched was less than the 1980 figure. You will recall that 1980 was the peak year during which six new classes of submarines and large surface combatants appeared. The lower number of overall launches in 1982 (compared to 1980) was due to many factors, including transition to new, more sophisticated designs, and less than one for one replacement.

The Soviets launched the fourth, and probably last, KIEV class aircraft carrier in 1982. The other three are now assigned to the Northern, Pacific, and Black Sea Fleets.

With the last of the KIEV class carriers completed, I believe the Soviets will now devote more effort to building their first aircraft carrier with catapults and arresting gear. Shipyard improvements and other indicators all point to the continued development of a conventional take-off and landing carrier program.

The Soviets are currently completing improvements to Nikolayev Shipyard on the Black Sea, the shipyard that built the KIEV class carriers. These improvements would support construction of a large aircraft carrier. Long lead time items such as the power plant are believed to be in production at this time.

We expect the carrier will be operational by about 1990. It probably will be about 300 meters long with a displacement of about 60,000 tons. It will almost certainly be nuclear powered, and able to support an air group of about 60 fixed-wind aircraft and helicopters.

In other Soviet naval surface force developments, the second and probably last ship of the KIROV class nuclear-powered guided missile cruiser was fitting out in 1982, with sea trials expected this year. The weapons improvements on this second ship are so extensive that it could be called KIROV II. When fully operational, the two KIROV class cruisers will give the Soviet Navy better defenses against air or missile attacks.

With much the same armament, but about half the displacement, a new guided missile cruiser the Soviets are building in the Crimea on the Black Sea is an excellent complement to the KIROV. We call it KRASINA. It is a multipurpose ship armed with antisubmarine, antiship, and air defense weapons.

The SOVREMENNYY guided-missile destroyer class, first appearing in 1980 on sea trials in the Baltic, is best suited for anti-surface ship warfare. In fact, it was the first large modern Soviet combatant built without significant ASW weaponry. It carries 130mm guns, the largest built for a Soviet ship since the 1950s. It also carries antiship cruise missiles.

Similar in size to SOVREMENNYY, the

UDALOY class guided-missile destroyer continues in series production. Unlike SOVREMENNYY, the UDALOY class is primarily for ASW, and will succeed its predecessors as the main ASW ship in an integrated Soviet task force. It carries the new HELIX ASW helicopter and possibly a new sonar.

GRISHA and KRIVAK class frigates are nearing the end of series production. Fitted mainly for ASW, these two classes now total about 85; three more GRISHAs may be under construction. We have not yet identified a follow-on frigate.

The 1982 surface shipbuilding program in the aggregate added large, heavily armed combatants to the Soviet fleet—a strong continuation in the construction of seven classes of large surface combatants begun in the last decade. The Soviets clearly are making a major effort to attain a surface force capable of going anywhere and competing on an equal footing with the U.S. Navy; and they are putting the same kind of effort into their submarine force.

The Soviets launched the second TYPHOON class SSBN last year, and others are believed to be under construction. The TYPHOON is an entirely new Soviet SSBN design. It is the largest submarine ever built and, like the earlier Soviet DELTA class, its missiles can reach most targets in the United States without leaving port or the sanctuary of home waters. It carries 20 MIRVed SS-NX-20 ballistic missiles.

After producing the first of the OSCAR class cruise-missile submarine in 1980, the Soviets launched one more in 1982. Twice as large as any previous Soviet SSGN, it is armed with 24 SS-N-19s, a new antiship supersonic cruise missile that is fired while submerged with a maximum range of about 250 miles. This is the same cruise missile carried by the KIROV.

Six ALFA class nuclear attack submarines are now operational. ALFA is the world's fastest (over 40 knots) and may also be the deepest diving submarine. ALFA also is unique in its use of a titanium alloy for the pressure hull.

More VICTOR III class nuclear attack submarines were produced in 1982. In terms both of numbers and operational assignments, VICTORs remain the backbone of the Soviet Navy's nuclear attack submarine force.

Finally, we expect to see a new class of attack submarine follow the VICTOR program, probably beginning this year or next.

The Soviet Navy is also developing a sea launched land attack cruise missile similar to the US TOMAHAWK, and expected to be operational this year.

To complement these submarine, surface combatant and weapon programs, the Soviets have a small but growing amphibious force. In 1982 they launched the second of the IVAN ROGOV class LPDs, and completed additional ROPUCHA class LSTs. They also have the world's largest fleet of amphibious assault air cushion vehicles.

The Soviets are also continuing to work on their ability to replenish their ships while underway. In addition to the 25,000-ton replenishment ship BEREZINA, the Soviet Navy has about 30 AORs and AOs able to refuel warships alongside while underway; some of them can also transher solid stores. As a result, the amount of fuel provided by these oilers has increased from 65 percent of naval requirements in the early 1970s to about 80 percent today. Soviet technology for underway replenishment is nearly on a par with the best Western technology. Their operational experience is, however, spotty and we regularly see many Soviet ships refuel bow to stern, at slow speeds or at anchor.

In 1982, Soviet Naval Aviation continued to receive new BACKFIRE bombers. We expect the number of Soviet Naval Aviation BACKFIRE deliveries to increase steadily. The total number of FORGER VSTOL fighter-bombers available for KIEV class carriers also increased. Each KIEV normally carries 12 or 13 FORGERS and 14 to 17 HORMONE/HELIX helicopters. With these aircraft, Soviet Naval Aviation now can deliver a variety of weapons, for use in striking shipping, conducting ASW, or supporting amphibious operations.

Overall, then, the Soviet shipbuilding effort by the end of 1982 has resulted in a Navy with 4 KIEV carriers, 278 other major surface combatants, and 367 submarines.

The steady improvement made to Soviet naval shipyards in 1982 further underscores the USSR's commitment to building the most advanced and capable ships in the world. The Soviets have purposefully developed a huge but underused shipyard capacity, which includes five yards for submarine production, eight for large combatants, and about 20 others for auxiliaries and small combatants. A single yard, Severodvinsk, has more building positions for nuclear submarine construction than has the entire U.S. nuclear submarine construction program.

The USSR leads the world in many aspects of shipbuilding. The Soviets are the leaders in the marine application of gas turbines. They increasingly use the section method of construction, which reduces both building time and cost, and permits maximum use of each shipway. They lead in techniques for welding and have state-of-the-art metal cutting equipment. While the Soviets still have relative deficiencies in other aspects of shipbuilding, they have a first-rate overall industry. One additional sign of this is the increase in recent years of ship production for export, most notably KASHIN DDGs for India; FOXTROT class submarines for India, Cuda, and Libya; and the KONI class frigate designed expressly for foreign navies. Not since Moscow sold a cruiser and destroyers to Indonesia in the 1950s have we seen such large ships being built for export.

Large numbers of ships and shipyards do not, of themselves, make a country a naval power. It is the use of those naval forces which counts even more than numbers. The Soviets did use their Navy in 1982 and there were several new developments.

The Soviet operation which attracted the most attention was the simulated strike against two U.S. aircraft carriers last fall by Soviet naval BACKFIRE bombers in the western Pacific. On two occasions, BACKFIREs came within about 100 miles of U.S. carriers as part of the overall reaction to one of our exercises. While the Soviets routinely monitor such exercises and simulate various reactions, this was the first use of BACKFIREs against our carriers. It was also the first use of BACKFIRE over the open ocean in the Pacific.

In December, the Soviet carrier MINSK operating in the Indian Ocean launched FORGER VTOL aircraft in reaction to U.S. carrier operations. This activity represented the first time Soviet carrier aircraft have intercepted U.S. carrier aircraft. Our pilots stated the FORGER intercepts were not very polished. U.S. carrier pilots routinely practice these procedures; and the Soviets would probably like to do more such intercepts as opportunity permits.

Another important development was Shield '82, the largest Warsaw Pact exercise in the Balkans in at least a decade. The participation of the carrier KIEV was an interesting aspect. This was its first major amphibious exercise. The Soviets are showing a growing interest in the development of carrier based air support for landing forces and probably already are working on concepts for the employment of their new aircraft carriers.

During 1982, the Soviet Navy kept ships year around in the Mediterranean Sea, the Indian Ocean, the South Atlantic off West Africa, and the South China Sea, and conducted deployments to the Caribbean. Particularly noteworthy in this regard has been Soviet activity at the former U.S.

naval complex at Cam Ranh Bay, Viet Nam, to improve their operations in both the South China Sea and the Indian Ocean. There are now Soviet ships always in port at Cam Ranh; and Soviet naval BEAR aircraft routinely deploy to Cam Ranh airfield from where they regularly fly reconnaissance and ASW missions throughout the region.

The overall level of worldwide Soviet out-of-area operations has remained fairly stable since the mid-1970s, measured by ship-days. However, in areas where we once would expect to find a destroyer or frigate size combatant, we now see cruisers and even KIEV carriers. This reflects the Soviets' growing interest in strengthening their influence with Third World nations, as well as balancing deployed Western naval forces. The December 1982 port visit to Bombay by the carrier MINSK is an example of the kind of Soviet ship visits that we are seeing more and more as a matter of routine.

Soviet ocean surveillance in 1982 was marked by high level of activity in space based systems. The Soviets launched 107 satellites—the highest yearly total to date. All of these had military application and some were dedicated to ocean surveillance.

In addition to the expansion of their own naval capabilities, the Soviets continued in 1982 to export weaponry to Third World countries at the same high levels established in 1981. Weapons deliveries included such relatively sophisticated naval systems as diesel attack submarines, guided missile destroyers, frigates, and missile patrol boats.

For the second year in a row, Cuba remained the principal recipient of Soviet weaponry. In 1981 Cuba received the largest arount of arms since 1962; but the 1982 total was even higher. These massive deliveries allowed Cuban armed forces, and particularly the Cuban Navy, to continue a significant upgrade of their combat capabilities.

Cuba's missile patrol boats are a strong offensive force, especially against undefended shipping. The surface force has been further augmented by the acquisition of a Soviet KONI class frigate; we would expect Cuba to receive additional KONIs. The two FOXTROT submarines received in 1979 and 1980 give Havana an important long-range attack capability it has not had heretofore. We believe Cuba will receive additional submarines over the next few years. During 1982 the Cubans also received two Soviet POLNOCNY LSMs, providing them their first true amphibious capability. The upgrade of Cuban naval forces has been accompanied by a major expansion of Cuban naval facilities.

In conjunction with Havana's Air Force—the largest in Latin America after Brazil—the Cuban

A BACKFIRE B of Soviet Naval Aviation carrying a single AS-4 missile under the fuselage, photographed by the Swedish Air Force while flying over the Baltic. SNA operates about 100 of these supersonic strike aircraft.

Navy poses a credible offensive threat to U.S. forces in the Caribbean, a threat that did not exist as recently as four years ago.

In the Far East, North Korea has renewed its naval competition with South Korea, after a pause in the late 1970s to build up its merchant and fishing fleet. North Korea changed this concentration in 1980 in an attempt to widen its edge over the South, primarily in the vital category of surface-to-surface missile combatants. Highlights of this effort include the launching last year of a unique missile-armed frigate; new diesel attack submarines; and the addition of antiship cruise-missile launchers on smaller craft. North Korea now has several different classes of combatants under construction or modification.

This development underscores North Korea's intention to improve its capabilities for coastal defense, amphibious raids, and combat against both South Korea and U.S. naval units. Also, the buildup gives the North a greater patrol capability for its extended 200-mile economic zone and 50-mile military zone declared in 1977.

The Chinese Navy made news in 1982 with its first launching at sea of a submarine-launched ballistic missile. This event made China the fifth country to launch a missile from a submarine.

We often forget that China has the world's third largest navy. Most of its major combatants are less then 15 years old, and include an SSBN, two nuclear attack submarines, over 100 conventional submarines, 12 guided missile destroyers (with

SSMs), and 23 frigates. As China turns increasingly to the sea for oil and other resources, and as the Soviet naval presence increases in the Western Pacific, the Chinese have stepped up efforts to modernize and expand their naval capabilities. Despite these efforts, China will remain principally a regional naval power for the rest of the century.

Since January 1982 the Libyan Navy has added several new units as part of its expansion program: it acquired another FOXTROT submarine, one additional NANUCHKA missile boat and two more NATYA minesweepers from the Soviets. Seven LA COMBATTANTE missile boats were also acquired from France. While the Libyan Navy represents a growing and potentially dangerous force in the Mediterranean, it has deficiencies which prevent Qadhafi from exploiting fully its capabilities. Similar problems affect Libya's Air Force, while it continues to receive Soviet MIG fighters and BLINDER bombers. Qadhafi retains, however, the capability to launch air sorties against U.S. operations in the Mediterranean or in support of Libyan-backed insurgent forces in Chad or the Sudan.

Returning to a final comment on Soviet naval developments in 1982, I want to discuss a problem that grows more critical each day. That is the accelerating pace of Soviet acquisition of Western military technology. The Soviets have carried out a massive program to obtain, by legal and illegal means, the most advanced Western technology available. Those of us with specific responsibilities for protecting information are most enthusiastic about the attention the Congress has given to this problem.

Shortly before his death, Chairman Brezhenv emphasized the need to acquire military technology. At an October 1982 gathering of key Soviet military leaders, he stated, "Competition in military technology has sharply intensified, often acquiring a fundamentally new character. Lag in this competition is inadmissible. We expect that our scientists, designers, engineers and technicians will do everything possible to resolve successfully all tasks connected with this." Because of this emphasis, Western technology that has both civilian and military uses almost always finds its way into Soviet military industries first, and civilian industries later. We have seen that take place in everything from microelectronic manufacturing equipment to the Kama Truck Plant, which has produced large numbers of military vehicles now used by the Soviets in Afghanistan.

The means for technology transfer vary. Much information is obtained by the thousands of Soviet researchers and analysts who comb the pages of Western technical journals. Commercial channels, either open or clandestine, provide advanced equipment and know-how. Soviet Bloc intelligence services target defense contractors and high-technology firms. They also target international organizations with access to advanced technology that includes computer data base networks. Visiting Soviet Bloc technical and student delegations consist generallly of expert scientists, many of them engaged in military work at home. Soviet candidates in scientific exchange programs routinely request research assignments here for projects that have military applications. Simply attending high-technology trade fairs can help obtain useful information on emerging technologies before security restrictions may shut it off from the Soviet Bloc.

When I said earlier that the pace of technology transfer by the Soviets was accelerating, I had in mind the much shorter length of time it takes before they have our designs in place in their naval equipment. For example, the first integrated circuits appeared in the early 1970s, copied from U.S. devices some 10 years old. By the mid-decade, they were copying entire families of integrated circuits within two to four years of the time they appeared in U.S. catalogs. By the end of the decade, they could copy and manufacture our newest devices within about two years.

In sum, the transfer of Western technology to the Soviets is a serious growing problem. It has been a key part of Moscow's efforts to catch up in areas in which it lags, and to widen the gap in areas in which it has the lead. Where we once had an overwhelming qualitative technological edge, that edge is eroding rapidly. If a war ever occurred, we would find ourselves facing Soviet-built weapons at least partly developed with our own technology and tax dollars. Our Chief of Naval Operations, Admiral James D. Watkins, has described it as like "being in a tail chase with ourselves."

Overall Soviet naval developments in 1982 lead to several conclusions.

First, while we await more signs of the military policies to be followed by the Andropov regime, I do not anticipate any early changes of direction regarding the Soviet Navy. The Navy has been allocated approximately the same share of the total military budget for a number of years, so its growth has not been at the expense of other services. The Soviet decision just last year to end military draft deferments for all but a few students is only the most recent sign of a continued commitment to devote scarce resources, in this case manpower, to sustain military power.

The steady, year-after-year expansion of Soviet Navy capabilities shows no signs of slowing down. I think that the Soviets will probably maintain a fairly constant number of about 60 SSBNs well into the next decade, as the TYPHOON and is successor replace older classes. The overall number of general-purpose submarines will decline as obsolescent diesel submarines are retired, but the number of state-of-the-art nuclear-powered ones will increase. The number of principal surface warships will likely decline somewhat, but there will be more of the large, powerful ships.

We expect the Soviets to continue to use our technology and theirs to improve their cruise missiles, air defenses, and naval aviation. These developments will continue the trend of the last decade from a navy designed for a short, intense war toward a navy with a greater endurance, larger weapons loads, and extensive communication and electronic warfare systems. The Soviets seem to have taken to heart what I believe is a key lesson of history, which is that most wars last much longer than they are supposed to.

The primary wartime tasks of the Soviet Navy will continue to be protecting their SSBNs until they can strike, and defending the homeland from Western SSBNs and aircraft carriers. This would entail Soviet attempts to control in war all or part of the Kara, Barents, and Okhotsk Seas, and the Northwest Pacific Basin, and to conduct sea denial operations beyond those areas. As new Western long-range land-attack cruise missiles become operational, moreover, we expect the Soviet Navy to expand its sea denial operations.

At the same time, the greater ability to range farther at sea obviously increases the Soviet Navy's ability to operate against Western sea lanes. As the Soviets have thought more seriously about the possibility of a prolonged war, they have emphasized this role more. I might add that cutting off vital sea lanes is a measure that could be threatened for peacetime political leverage as well.

The Soviet Navy is becoming an increasingly valuable peacetime asset to the Soviet leadership. Al Capone reputedly once said, "You can get better results with a kind word and a gun, than with a kind word alone." The Soviets seem to follow this kind of maxim as they practice an aggressive naval diplomacy. We expect them to expand their level of operations in such areas as the Caribbean and Philippine Seas, West Africa and the southwest Indian Ocean islands. Given the likelihood of continued instability in the Third World, the opportunity for use of such naval diplomacy will undoubtedly increase.

This is not to say the Soviet Navy will alter its singular approach to materiel and crew readiness in discharging its assigned tasks. This approach, which is uniform throughout the Soviet armed forces, aims at ensuring maximum materiel availability in times of crisis through minimum day-to-day use. To the Soviets, it is more important to be ready to go to sea than actually to be at sea—a philosophy that explains why, on the average day, only about 15% of the Soviet Navy is deployed beyond home waters. Limiting material wear and tear is the rule even while on distant deployments. For example, during the November 1982-January 1983 deployment to the Caribbean, Soviet Navy ships spent 52 of the total 68 days in port.

Although the Soviet Navy's wartime tasks and approach to readiness should remain basically unchanged during the next decade, its capabilities to operate effectively in an expanding variety of circumstances over broader ocean areas will probably increase. We expect the quality of the Navy's materiel, maintenance, and personnel to further improve; its command and control system to become more responsive and survivable; and its ability to sustain combat operations to increase. Expansion of the Navy's support facilities and capabilities, advances in ocean surveillance systems, increasingly realistic training, and greater out-of-area operational experience all portend continuing improvement in the professionalism, maturity, and proficiency of the Soviet Navy.

In short, Admiral Gorshkov's goal of a "balanced fleet" is still being vigorously pursued. The Soviet Navy, which today poses a clear and present challenge to our national interests, will be even more capable tomorrow. The stronger it becomes relative to our own Navy, the less restrained the leaders of the Andropov regime need be in their political and military diplomacy. This is the growing danger we confront.

An artist's concept of the new Soviet BLACKJACK strike aircraft, which is expected to enter service with Soviet Naval Aviation and strategic aviation in the late 1980s. This four-engine, variable-geometry-wing aircraft will pose a potent threat to Western shipping.

Appendix B. SOVIET NAVY ORDER OF BATTLE
(June 1983)

1. Active Ships

Submarines—Nuclear Propelled

SSBN*	Modern Ballistic Missile Submarines (YANKEE, DELTA, TYPHOON)	62
SSBN	Older Ballistic Missile Submarines (HOTEL)	4
SSGN*	Cruise Missile Submarines (ECHO II, CHARLIE, PAPA, OSCAR, YANKEE)	50**
SSN*	Torpedo Attack Submarines (NOVEMBER, ECHO I, VICTOR, ALFA, YANKEE) .	60**

Submarines—Diesel-electric Propelled

SSB	Older Ballistic Missile Submarines (GOLF)	15
SSG	Cruise Missile Submarines (WHISKEY, JULIETT)	20
SS	Torpedo Attack Submarines (WHISKEY, ZULU, ROMEO, FOXTROT, TANGO, KILO) .	149
SSAG	Special-purpose Submarines (INDIA, LIMA)	3
SSQ	Communications Submarines (GOLF)	3
SSR	Radar Picket Submarines (WHISKEY)	1
SST	Training Submarines (BRAVO)	4

Aviation Ships

CVHG*	VTOL Carriers (KIEV)	3
CHG	Helicopter Cruisers (MOSKVA)	2

Cruisers

CGN*	Guided Missile Cruisers (Nuclear) (KIROV)	1
CG*	Guided Missile Cruisers (SVERDLOV, KYNDA, KRESTA I/II, KARA, KRASINA)................	28
CL	Light Cruisers (SVERDLOV) .	9

Destroyers

DDG*	Guided Missile Destroyers	40
DD	Destroyers	25

Frigates (Escorts)

FFG*	Guided Missile Frigates (KRIVAK)	32
FF	Frigates	35
FFL*	Light Frigates	110
Small Combatants*		150

Amphibious Warfare Ships

LPD	Dock Landing Ships	2
LST	Tank Landing Ships	28
LSM	Medium Landing Ships.......	55
Mine Warfare Ships*.................		145
Mine Warfare Craft*..................		260
Intelligence Collection Ships*		55

Auxiliary Ships*

Underway Replenishment Ships........	80
Support Ships......................	70
Tug-Salvage-Rescue Ships	145
Other Auxiliary Types................	430

---

*Indicates additional units under construction.

**Several YANKEE-class SSBNs are being converted to SSN/SSGN configurations.

2. Active Aircraft (including helicopters)

Strike/Bombers
   (BACKFIRE, BADGER, BLINDER) ... 370

Fighter-Attack
   (FITTER, FORGER) 100

Tankers (BADGER) 75

Reconnaissance/Electronic Warfare
   (BADGER, BEAR D, BLINDER,
   CUB, COOT) 170

Antisubmarine Warfare
   (BEAR F, HAZE, HELIX, HORMONE
   A, MAIL, MAY) 445

Utility/Transport/Training............. 375
                                    ───────
                                     1,500+

3. Active Naval Personnel

Afloat.............................186,000
Shore Support 123,000
Naval Aviation 68,000
Training 57,000
Coastal Defense 14,000
Naval Infantry (marines) 13,000
                                    ───────
                                    461,000

This foredeck view of the new nuclear powered missile cruiser, KIROV, reveals the high density of weapons carried. From left to right can be seen the circular "manhole" covers of the SA-N-4 missile launchers on the 02 level, the 20 large hatch areas for the launchers of a new type antiship cruise missile; the 12 smaller covers for the new vertical launch SA-N-6 missile system (each of which covers a separate rotating magazine loaded with a number of missiles); lastly, 4 of the 8 30mm-Gatling guns can be seen on the deck houses on either side of the large missile hatches.

Appendix C. SOVIET WARSHIP DESCRIPTIONS

Our Navy is a focal point for the most recent achievements of science and technology. Nuclear missiles, powerful propulsion plants, and radar and electronic equipment have given it new qualities and advanced the Navy into the rank of forces of strategic significance.

Fleet Admiral N.I. SMIRNOV
First Deputy Commander-in-Chief
Soviet Navy

This appendix provides basic descriptive data and photographs of the more significant Soviet submarines and surface ships.

Arrangements: Submarine classes are arranged alphabetically, followed by surface combatants arranged generally by size and lastly the amphibious ships.

Classification: The dimensions, characteristics, and general information are approximate.

Designations: Simplified ship designations have been used in this appendix; they are not necessarily the formal designations assigned by U.S./NATO navies. All ships' class names are NATO code names except those indicated by asterisks, which are transliterations of the actual Soviet names.

More complete data on Soviet ships and aircraft, as well as a comprehensive discussion of the development of the contemporary Soviet fleet, are provided in Norman Polmar, *Guide to the Soviet Navy*/3rd Edition (Annapolis, Md.: Naval Institute Press, 1983).

The Soviets do not necessarily classify their ships as we do in the West. Following are a sampling of the transliterations from Russian of Soviet ships types, with their English meanings and the classes so identified:

BDK —BOL'SHOY DESANTNYY KORABL' = Large Landing Ship (IVAN ROGOV, ALLIGATOR)

BPK —BOL'SHOY PROTIVOLODOCHNYY KORABL' = Large Antisubmarine Ship (KARA, KRESTA II)

EM —ESAKDRENNYY MINONOSETS = Fleet Destroyer Ship (KOTLIN)

MPK—MALYY PROTIVOLODOCHNYY KORABL' = Small Antisubmarine Ship (GRISHA, MIRKA)

PKR —PROTIVOLODOCHNYY KREYSER = Antisubmarine Cruiser (MOSKVA)

PLA —PODVODNAYA LODKA ATOMNAYA = Submarine, Nuclear (VICTOR, NOVEMBER)

RKR —RAKETNYY KREYSER = Missile Cruiser (KYNDA, KRESTA I)

SK —STOROZHEVOY KORABL' = Escort Ship (KRIVAK)

SUBMARINES

ALFA attack submarine

Nuclear Powered Attack Submarine (SSN): ALFA class

Displacement:	2,800 tons surfaced
	3,680 tons submerged
Length:	80 meters (262 feet)
Propulsion:	Nuclear
Main Armament:	torpedoes, probably ASW missiles

The ALFA class SSN is the latest in the line of Soviet nuclear powered attack submarines. The hull, made of light-weight, non-magnetic titanium, is the most streamlines hull shape ever produced by the Soviets, suggesting that this submarine was designed to maximize speed, which is estimated to be at least 43 knots. This is a small, high technology submarine with a very deep diving ability and probably is fitted with advanced weapons. The Soviets have been pursuing this program for a number of years and have several units of the ALFA class with an improved titanium reported to be under construction.

BRAVO training submarine

Training Submarine (SST): BRAVO class

Displacement:	2,400 tons surfaced
	2,900 tons submerged
Length:	73 meters (240 feet)
Propulsion:	Diesel-electric
Main Armament:	torpedo tubes possible

The BRAVO class SSTs entered the Soviet Navy in the late 1960s as target and training submarines. Only four units were produced. Although they are not viewed primarily as "attack" submarines, they may be armed with torpedoes.

CHARLIE I cruise missile submarine

Nuclear Powered Cruise Missile Submarine (SSGN): CHARLIE I class

Displacement:	4,000 tons surfaced
	4,900 tons submerged
Length:	95 meters (313 feet)
Propulsion:	Nuclear
Main Armament:	8 SS-N-7 antiship missiles
	torpedo tubes

The first unit of this class became operational in 1967. Their SS-N-7 submarine launched antiship cruise missiles have a range of more than 55 kilometers (30 nautical miles). About twelve CHARLIE I SSGNs were built before being succeeded by the improved CHARLIE II program. One CHARLIE-class submarine was lost with about 90 crewmen off Kamchatka in mid-1983.

CHARLIE II cruise missile submarine

Nuclear Powered Cruise Missile Submarine (SSGN): CHARLIE II class

Displacement:	4,300 tons surfaced
	5,100 tons submerged
Length:	103 meters (340 feet)
Propulsion:	Nuclear
Main Armament:	8 SS-N-7 or SS-N-9 antiship missiles
	torpedo tubes

This is an improved CHARLIE II class SSGN. The larger size may accommodate an increased weapons and sensors capability. If the SS-N-9 is carried, it would improve this submarine's missile capability, including an extension of range to probably twice that of the 30 mile range of the SS-N-7. Seven units were completed from 1973 to 1982.

Nuclear Powered Ballistic Missile Submarine (SSBN): DELTA I class

Displacement: 9,000 tons surfaced
                                         11,750 tons submerged
Length: 140 meters (462 feet)
Propulsion: Nuclear
Main Armament: 12 SS-N-8 strategic SLBMs
                                       torpedo tubes

The DELTA class SSBNs are follow-on submarines to the YANKEE class. The first DELTA I went to sea in 1972. This SSBN carries 12 SS-N-8 SLBMs with a range of more than 7,500 kilometers (4,000 nautical miles). These missiles allow Soviet DELTAs to remain in range of most North American targets while in home waters. Eighteen DELTA Is were completed through 1977.

Nuclear Powered Ballistic Missile Submarine (SSBN): DELTA II class

Displacement: 10,000 tons surfaced
                                         12,750 submerged
Length: 155 meters (511 feet)
Propulsion: Nuclear
Main Armament: 16 SS-N-8 strategic SLBMs
                                       torpedo tubes

The DELTA II class, a lengthened version of the DELTA I, was first deployed in the Soviet Northern Fleet in early 1976. Other than its greater length and larger missile battery, the DELTA II is similar to the DELTA I SSBN. Only four were completed in 1974-1975.

DELTA III ballistic missile submarine

Nuclear Powered Ballistic Missile Submarine (SSBN): DELTA III class

Displacement:	10,500 tons surfaced
	13,250 tons submerged
Length:	155 meters (512 feet)
Propulsion:	Nuclear
Main Armament:	16 SS-N-18 strategic SLBMs
	torpedo tubes

The DELTA III SSBNs are a follow-on to the DELTA II, and are similar in most respects, except for their more advanced, MIRV capable SS-N-18 missile. This weapon has a range of approximately 5,000 nautical miles. The missile compartment is higher in the DELTA III than in the DELTA II to accommodate the longer SS-N-18. Fourteen were built through 1983 with some additional hulls reported.

ECHO attack submarine

Nuclear Powered Attack Submarine (SSN): ECHO class

Displacement:	4,500 tons surfaced
	5,500 tons submerged
Length:	110 meters (363 feet)
Propulsion:	Nuclear
Main Armament:	torpedo tubes

Five ECHO I class cruise missile submarines (SSGN) were built from 1960 to 1962. These submarines were originally armed with six tubes for the SS-N-3 SHADDOCK cruise missile plus torpedo tubes. All five units have now been converted to an attack configuration (SSN) by removal of the missile tubes. Torpedoes now comprise their weapons capability. As SSNs, this class is known simply as ECHO without the suffix "I." It was a submarine of this class which had an internal accident off Okinawa in August 1980. A number of her crew were killed or injured; the submarine had to be towed to Vladivostok.

Nuclear Powered Cruise Missile Submarine (SSGN): ECHO II class

Displacement:	5,000 tons surfaced
	6,000 tons submerged
Length:	115 meters (379 feet)
Propulsion:	Nuclear
Main Armament:	8 SS-N-3/12 antiship cruise missiles
	torpedo tubes

Twenty-nine ECHO II class SSGNs were completed between 1962 and 1967. All are in active Soviet service. These submarines are armed with eight SS-N-3 (and in some, SS-N-12) cruise missiles plus torpedo tubes. These submarines must surface to fire their missiles. The maximum effective range of the SS-N-3 missile in the antiship role is about 375 kilometers (250 nautical miles), however, the missile is capable of significantly longer aerodynamic flight. The submarine must rely on some outside source for targeting information when firing its missiles beyond visual/radar range of the submarine. For many years the ECHO II has been one of the primary anticarrier threats. Units of this class frequently deploy to the Mediterranean Sea.

FOXTROT attack submarines

Attack Submarine (SS): FOXTROT class

Displacement:	1,950 tons surfaced
	2,400 tons submerged
Length:	91 meters (300 feet)
Propulsion:	Diesel-electric
Main Armament:	torpedo tubes

The FOXTROT is a popular fleet-type attack submarine introduced in the late 1950s and still widely used. Eight have been provided to India, several to Libya, and two to Cuba. About 60 remain active in the Soviet Navy. The Soviets routinely deploy units of this class to the Mediterranean Sea and Indian Ocean and on occasion to the Caribbean.

GOLF command and control submarine

Command and Control Submarine (SSQ): GOLF class

Displacement:	2,300 tons surfaced
	2,700 tons submerged
Length:	100 meters (330 feet)
Propulsion:	Diesel-electric
Main Armament:	torpedo tubes

The GOLF class SSQ is a recent conversion of the GOLF I class SSB. The missiles have been removed and a variety of communication antennas have been installed, suggesting the submarines will perform some command, control, and communication function. The submarines probably retains its torpedo-firing capability. At least three submarines have been connected to this configuration.

GOLF ballistic missile submarine

Ballistic Missile Submarine (SSB): GOLF I/II classes

Displacement:	2,300 tons surfaced
	2,700 tons submerged
Length:	100 meters (330 feet)
Propulsion:	Diesel-electric
Main Armament:	3 SS-N-4 or 3 SS-N-5 SLBMs
	torpedo tubes

Twenty-three GOLF diesel ballistic missile submarines (SSB) were built from 1958 to 1962, one of which accidentally sank in the mid-Pacific in 1967. The submarines were built to carry three SS-N-4 Submarine Launched Ballistic Missiles (SLBM). These SLBMs were launched while the submarine was surfaced and had an estimated range of over 600 kilometers (325 nautical miles). Many of these submarines were modified to the GOLF II configuration carrying the SS-N-5 SERB SLBM with estimated range of 1,300 kilometers (700 nautical miles), and can launch their missiles while submerged. About 15 units, mostly GOLF IIs, are still in active service with six of them based in the Baltic.

One GOLF was converted to a test platform for the SS-N-8 submarine-launched ballistic missile (GOLF III), one for the SS-N-6 (GOLF IV), and one for the SS-N-20 (GOLF V).

Nuclear Powered Ballistic Missile Submarine (SSBN): HOTEL II/III classes

Displacement:	5,000 tons surfaced
	6,000 tons submerged
Length:	115 meters (379 feet)
Propulsion:	Nuclear
Main Armament:	3 SS-N-5 SLBMs
	torpedo tubes

Eight of the HOTEL SSBN class were completed from 1958 to 1962. Initially the submarines carried three surface launched SS-N-4 missiles. Their conversion to the HOTEL II configuration replaced the SS-N-4 with the submerged-launched SS-N-5. One HOTEL (now designated HOTEL III) has been modified to a missile test submarine for the SS-N-8 SLBM.

INDIA Class SSAG

Auxiliary Submarine (SSAG): INDIA Class

Displacement:	3,200 tons surfaced
	4,000 tons submerged
Length:	106 meters (349 feet)
Propulsion:	Diesel-electric
Main Armament:	Probably torpedo tubes

The INDIA is a search and rescue submarine and carries two submersible vehicles nested in wells aft of the sail.

Cruise Missile Submarine (SSG): JULIETT class

Displacement:	3,000 tons surfaced
	3,750 tons submerged
Length:	90 meters (297 feet)
Propulsion:	Diesel-electric
Main Armament:	4 SS-N-3 antiship missiles
	torpedo tubes

Sixteen JULIETT submarines were built during the early 1960s. The JULIETT is fitted with four tubes for the SS-N-3 antiship cruise missile which is a surface-launched weapon of about 250nm range. As with the ECHO II class, over-the-horizon targeting must be accomplished with outside sources. All 16 submarines are believed to be in active service. Units are frequently deployed to the Mediterranean Sea.

Attack Submarine (SS): KILO class

Displacement:	2,500 tons surfaced
	3,200 tons submerged
Length:	67 meters (221 feet)
Propulsion:	Diesel-electric
Main Armament:	torpedo tubes

This is a medium-range submarine, apparently intended to replace the outdated WHISKEY and ROMEO classes. They may also be intended for foreign transfer. The first KILO was completed in 1982 with additional units reported under construction.

Auxiliary Submarine (SSAG): LIMA class

The LIMA Class is a new small submarine probably intended for research purposes.

Nuclear Powered Attack Submarine (SSN): NOVEMBER class

Displacement:	4,500 tons surfaced
	5,300 tons submerged
Length:	110 meters (363 feet)
Propulsion:	Nuclear
Main Armament:	torpedo tubes

The NOVEMBER SSN, the first Soviet nuclear powered submarine, became operational in 1958. Fourteen units were completed by 1965. One NOVEMBER sank in the eastern Atlantic in April of 1970 (pictured above; the crew was removed before sinking). The NOVEMBER class submarines are armed with torpedoes and, as most attack submarines, can also carry mines. Submarines of this class pioneered Soviet operations under the Arctic pack ice.

OSCAR cruise missile submarine (fitting out at Severodvinsk)

Nuclear Powered Cruise Missile Submarine (SSGN): OSCAR class

Displacement:	10,000 tons surfaced
	14,000 tons submerged
Length:	143 meters (472 feet)
Propulsion:	Nuclear; approximately 30 knots
Main Armament:	24 SS-N-19 missiles
	torpedo tubes

These are the most heavily armed general-purpose submarines yet constructed by any nation, with 24 tubes for submerged-launch. Long-range (over 250 nautical miles) anti-ship missiles plus torpedo tubes. The OSCAR is the largest non-strategic missile (SSBN) submarine ever built. The first OSCAR was completed in 1982.

PAPA cruise missile submarine

Nuclear Powered Cruise Missile Submarine (SSGN): PAPA class

Displacement:	6,700 tons surfaced
	7,500 tons submerged
Length:	109 meters (360 feet)
Propulsion:	Nuclear; 35-40 knots
Main Armament:	10 SS-N-9 missiles
	torpedo tubes

A single PAPA-class SSGN was built, being the prototype for the larger OSCAR series. The submarine has an advanced propulsion plant. The single PAPA was completed in 1970.

ROMEO attack submarine

Attack Submarine (SS): ROMEO class

Displacement:	1,330 tons surfaced
	1,700 tons submerged
Length:	77 meters (254 feet)
Propulsion:	Diesel-electric
Main Armament:	torpedo tubes

About 20 ROMEO class submarines were completed between 1958 and 1961. Built along WHISKEY class lines, ROMEOs probably have improved ASW capabilities over the WHISKEY. Six of these submarines have been transferred to Egypt, two to Bulgaria, and a number have been built in China (PRC) and North Korea. The ROMEO class submarines have eight torpedo tubes and can launch mines as well as torpedoes.

TANGO attack submarine

Attack Submarine (SS): TANGO class

Displacement:	3,000 tons surfaced
	3,700 tons submerged
Length:	91 meters (300 feet)
Propulsion:	Diesel-electric
Main Armament:	torpedo tubes (probably ASW missiles)

The TANGO is a modern diesel-electric powered, torpedo-attack submarine. This submarine continues in series production and reflects the most modern diesel-electric technology. It has a long endurance when submerged and operates quietly on batteries. The first TANGO became operational in 1973, and a number of units have been constructed, demonstrating the Soviet Navy's continued interest in advanced diesel submarines. Units of this class frequently deploy to the Mediterranean.

TYPHOON ballistic missile submarine

Nuclear Powered Ballistic Missile Submarine (SSBN): TYPHOON class

Displacement:	approximately 25,000 tons submerged
Length:	170 meters (561 feet)
Propulsion:	Nuclear; approximately 30 knots
Main Armament:	20 SS-N-20 strategic SLBMs
	torpedo tubes

The TYPHOON is the largest undersea craft to be constructed by any nation. It appears to have two internal pressure hulls within a single outer hull structure. Several features indicate that the TYPHOON was intended to operate under the Arctic ice pack. The first TYPHOON submarine was completed in 1983 with a second submarine also launched that year.

Nuclear Powered Attack Submarine (SSN): VICTOR I class

Displacement:	4,300 tons surfaced
	5,100 tons submerged
Length:	95 meters (313 feet)
Propulsion:	Nuclear, over 30 knots submerged
Main Armament:	torpedo tubes

The first VICTOR class SSN was completed in 1967. This high-speed attack submarine was developed as a next generation to the NOVEMBER class, representing significant Soviet qualitative improvement in nuclear submarine design. The armament of the VICTOR consists of torpedoes and possibly antisubmarine missiles. This submarine class is one of the fastest in the world. Sixteen of this version were built.

VICTOR II attack submarine

Nuclear Powered Attack Submarine (SSN): VICTOR II class

Displacement:	4,500 tons surfaced
	5,700 tons submerged
Length:	100 meters (330 feet)
Propulsion:	Nuclear, over 30 knots submerged
Main Armament:	torpedo tubes and
	probably antisubmarine missiles

These submarines represent an improved follow-on of the VICTOR I class. They are slightly larger than the VICTOR I and probably have improved weapons and sensor fits. These submarines probably carry a submerged launched antisubmarine missile system similar to our SUBROC. It is reported that the Soviets have produced even another variant of the VICTOR. In one form or another, the VICTORs continued to be built and are the "backbone" of the Soviets nuclear attack submarine force. Seven were built.

Nuclear Powered Attack Submarine (SSN): VICTOR III class

Displacement:	4,600 tons surfaced
	5,800 tons submerged
Length:	106 meters (350 feet)
Propulsion:	Nuclear
Main Armament:	torpedo tubes and
	antisubmarine missiles

This third variation of the VICTOR design has more advanced weapons and sensor systems. A large pod is fitted atop the upper rudder to carry a towed passive sonar array. The first of at least 15 submarines of this type was completed in 1978 with construction continuing.

WHISKEY attack submarine

Attack Submarine (SS): WHISKEY class

Displacement:	1,050 tons surfaced
	1,350 tons submerged
Length:	75 meters (247 feet)
Propulsion:	Diesel-electric
Main Armament:	torpedo tubes

The design of the medium-range WHISKEY class SS was based extensively on later German World War II design concepts. A total of 236 submarines of this class were built during the 1950s in what was the largest submarine construction program of the post-World War II period. A number of units remain in Soviet active and reserve service, with some 40 to 50 submarines serving in the navies of Albania, Bulgaria, China (PRC), Egypt, Indonesia, North Korea, Cuba, and Poland. WHISKEY submarines are armed with six torpedo tubes. The various deck guns mounted in early variants have been removed from the surviving units. Modifications include CANVAS BAG radar picket submarine (SSR), and the TWIN CYLINDER and LONG BIN surfaced launched missile variations (SSG) carrying the SS-N-3 antiship or tactical nuclear missiles.

YANKEE ballistic missile submarine

Nuclear Powered Ballistic Submarine (SSBN): YANKEE I class

Displacement:	8,000 tons surfaced
	9,600 tons submerged
Length:	130 meters (429 feet)
Propulsion:	Nuclear
Main Armament:	16 SS-N-6 Strategic SLBMs
	torpedo tubes

The YANKEE I class, which became operational in 1968, was the first modern design SSBN in the Soviet Navy. A total of 34 submarines of this class was built. The YANKEE has 16 missile tubes for the SS-N-6 liquid fueled ballistic missile. There are three variants of the missile with ranges up to 2,950 kilometers (1,600 nautical miles). Some have MRV warheads. The SS-N-17 is a longer-range, solid fuel, more capable missile which is fitted in the YANKEE II variant of this class. To date only one YANKEE II has been so fitted. In order to keep within the limits of the SALT I agreement with the U.S., as each new DELTA or TYPHOON SSBN joins the fleet, an older YANKEE I class SSBN has its missile tubes removed.

ZULU attack submarine

Attack Submarine (SS): ZULU class

Displacement:	1,950 tons surfaced
Length:	90 meters (295 feet)
Propulsion:	Diesel-electric
Main Armament:	torpedo tubes
	(SSB version carries two
	SS-N-4 SLBMs in sail)

Twenty-six ZULU class submarines were produced from 1952 to 1955. The ZULU is longer ranged than the WHISKEY class of the same period and is fitted with more torpedo tubes. Several modifications were made, including the ZULU V, armed with two SS-N-4 ballistic missiles, which made them the first submarines in the world to carry ballistic missiles. Six ZULU hulls were completed as, or converted to, SSBs, but none remain in that configuration. The others reverted to SS status. ZULUs have been used in conjunction with research ships on extended oceanographic expeditions throughout the worlds oceans. About 11 remain in Soviet naval service.

AVIATION SHIPS

KIEV aircraft carrier

Guided Missile VTOL Aircraft Carrier (CVHG): KIEV class

Displacement:	38,000 tons full load
Length:	273 meters (901 feet)
Propulsion:	steam turbines, over 30 knots
Main Armament:	4 twin SS-N-12 launchers
	2 twin SA-N-3 SAM launchers (GOBLET)
	2 twin SA-N-4 SAM launchers
	1 twin SUW-N-1 ASW launcher
	2 twin 76mm dual purpose (DP) gun mounts
	8 single 30mm Gatling guns
	12 or 13 YAK-36 FORGER VTOL aircraft
	14 to 17 KA-25 HORMONE or KA-27 HELIX helicopters

The KIEV is the largest combatant class yet built in the Soviet Union. KIEV became operational in 1976, MINSK in 1978, a third unit in 1981, and another is under construction. This ship is considered the first Soviet "aircraft carrier," with the flexibility to deploy a mix of fixed and rotary-wing aircraft for a number of missions. Weapons include eight surface-to-surface cruise missile tubes, two twin SA-N-3 and two SA-N-4 SAM launchers, two 76-mm twin gun mounts, and eight "Gatling" guns. This is the first class since the KYNDA class CG which carries reloads for its surface-to-surface missile system. For ASW the ship has a twin antisubmarine missile launcher, two antisubmarine rocket launchers, and torpedo tubes as well as hull-mounted and variable-depth sonars. The KIEV class features a starboard "island" superstructure and an angled flight deck. The lack of catapults and arresting gear limits the KIEV to operating helicopters and Vertical Short Take Off and Landing (VSTOL) aircraft. Aircraft observed aboard the class to date are the FORGER A and B as well as HORMONE A/B/C variants. It is estimated the ship can carry 35 to 40 aircraft depending on the mix of VSTOL aircraft and helicopter embarked.

Ships of the class are: KIEV, MINSK, NOVOROSSIYSK, and KHARKOV.

Guided Missile Aviation Cruiser (CHG): MOSKVA* class

Displacement:	17,000 tons full load
Length:	189 meters (623 feet)
Propulsion:	steam turbines, 30 knots
Main Armament:	2 twin SA-N-3 SAM launchers (GOBLET)
	1 twin SUW-N-1 ASW launcher
	2 twin 57mm AA gun mounts
Aircraft:	18 KA-25 HORMONE helicopters

The MOSKVA and the LENINGRAD were completed in 1967 and 1968, respectively. The unique design of the ships includes a guided missile cruiser configuration forward and helicopter deck aft. There is a hangar deck below the flight deck which is serviced by two aircraft elevators. The MOSKVA class weapons suit includes twin antiaircraft and antisubmarine missile launchers, antisubmarine rockets, and torpedo tubes. The ships have hull-mounted and variable-depth sonars. They can carry about 18 HORMONE helicopters, with most or all normally configured for ASW. Both ships are home based in the Black Sea Fleet and operate regularly with the Mediterranean squadron.

Ships of the class are: MOSKVA and LENINGRAD.

SURFACE COMBATANTS

KIROV nuclear powered guided missile cruiser

Nuclear Powered Guided Missile Cruiser (CGN): KIROV class

Displacement:	28,000 tons full load
Length:	248 meters (818 feet)
Propulsion:	nuclear with fossil-fueled auxiliary, over 30 knots
Main Armament:	20 new type cruise missiles
	12 vertical SA-N-6 launchers
	2 twin SA-N-4 SAM launchers
	2 twin SS-N-14 ASW missile launchers with reloads
	2 single 100mm dual purpose gun mounts
	8 single 30mm Gatling guns
Aircraft:	several HORMONE helicopters
	with elevator and hangar deck aft

The KIROV is the Soviets' first nuclear powered surface warship. This ship had been under construction in Baltic Yard in Leningrad for a number of years and a second of the class will probably be launched within the year. After running sea trails in the Baltic through the summer of 1980 KIROV joined the Northern Fleet. This is the largest warship (other than aircraft carriers) built in the world since the end of World War II. Besides its large and varied weapons fit (which also includes torpedoes and ASW rockets) this ship is equipped with a vast array of electronics sensors and equipment including a new type large variable depth sonar, which is trailed from the stern door. The new cruise missiles are thought to be improvements over the SS-N-3/SS-N-12 family and the new SAM system may be a seaborne derivative of the ground based SA-X-10 missile system. A second ship was completed in 1983 and a third ship is under construction.

Guided Missile Cruiser (CG): SLAVA class

Displacement:	12,500 tons full load
Length:	187 meters (617 feet)
Propulsion:	gas turbines, over 30 knots
Main Armament:	8 twin SS-N-12 missile launchers
	8 vertical SA-N-6 missile launchers
	1 twin 130mm DP gun mount
	8 single 30mm Gatling guns
Aircraft:	1 or 2 KA-25 HORMONE-B helicopter

One of the latest warships to emerge from Soviet shipyards is the missile cruiser SLAVA, formerly designated KRASINA and before that BLACK-COM-1 by NATO intelligence. The 12,500-ton SLAVA's main battery consists of 16 SS-N-12 cruise missile tubes, each capable of firing a missile with more than twice the payload of the U.S. Tomahawk antiship missile. The ship also has advanced antiaircraft missiles and a nominal ASW capability.

KARA guided missile cruiser

Guided Missile Cruiser (CG): KARA class

Displacement:	9,700 tons full load
Length:	173 meters (571 feet)
Propulsion:	gas turbines, 32 knots
Main Armament:	2 quad SS-N-14 ASW missile launchers
	(SILEX) (no reloads)
	2 twin SA-N-3 SAM launchers (GOBLET)
	2 twin SA-N-4 SAM launchers
	2 twin 76mm DP gun mounts
	4 single 30mm Gatling guns
Aircraft:	1 KA-25 HORMONE helicopter

The KARA is one of the newest of Soviet guided missile cruiser classes. This is a highly capable, heavily armed warship, first seen at sea in 1973. The KARA weapons consist of eight tubes for the SS-N-14 antisubmarine missile, ten torpedo tubes, and antisubmarine rocket launchers plus dual purpose guns and surface-to-air missiles. A helicopter hangar and platform are fitted aft. Seven ships of this class are currently operational, with construction of the class probably complete. One unit, the AZOV, is extensively modified aft and is estimated to be the test platform for a new SAM system, probably to be installed on one or more of the four new major combatant classes.

The ships of this class are: AZOV, KERCH, NIKOLAYEV, OCHAKOV, PETROPAVLOVSK, TALLIN and TASHKENT.

Guided Missile Cruiser (CG): KRESTA I class

Displacement:	7,600 tons full load
Length:	155 meters (513 feet)
Propulsion:	steam turbines, 32 knots
Main Armament:	2 twin SS-N-3 SSMs launchers
	(no reloads)
	2 twin SA-N-1 SAM launchers (GOA)
	2 twin 57mm AA gun mounts
Aircraft:	1 KA-25 HORMONE helicopter

The KRESTA I cruiser is slightly smaller than the KRESTA II. It is a versatile and heavily armed ship with antiship cruise missile tubes, two antiaircraft missile launchers, guns, ten torpedo tubes, antisubmarine weapons, and a helicopter platform with hangar. The KRESTA I was the first Soviet combatant to have a helicopter hangar. Four units of this class were completed prior to development of the KRESTA II follow-on design. One ship has been fitted with four rapid-fire "Gatling" guns. The SS-N-3 surface-to-surface cruise missiles carried by this class are estimated to be capable of delivering either a nuclear or high explosive warhead over a distance of about 250nm. No reloads are provided on board for this weapon.

The ships of this class are: ADMIRAL ZOZULYA, SEVASTOPOL, VITSE ADMIRAL DROZD, and VLADIVOSTOK.

Guided Missile Cruiser (CG): KRESTA II class

Displacement:	7,700 tons full
Length:	159 meters (524 feet)
Propulsion:	steam turbines, 32 knots
Main Armament:	1 quad SS-N-14 ASW missile launchers (SILEX) (no reloads)
	2 twin SA-N-3 SAM launchers (GOBLET)
	2 twin 57mm AA gun mounts
Aircraft:	1 KA-25 HORMONE helicopter

The first KRESTA II cruiser became operational about 1970. These ships are armed with eight tubes for the 30nm range SS-N-14 antisubmarine missile, twin antiaircraft missiles launchers, four 57-mm AA and four "Gatling" antiaircraft guns, ten torpedo tubes, antisubmarine weapons, and a helicopter platform with hangar. Ten ships of this class are operational. Ships of this class are: ADMIRAL ISACHENKOV, ADMIRAL ISAKOV, ADMIRAL MAKAROV, ADMIRAL NAKHIMOV, ADMIRAL OKTYABR'SKIY, ADMIRAL YUMASHEV, KRONSHTADT, MARSHAL TIMOSHENKO, MARSHAL VOROSHILOV, and VASILY CHAPAYEV.

Guided Missile Cruiser (CG): KYNDA class

Displacement:	5,500 tons full load
Length:	142 meters (468 feet)
Propulsion:	steam turbine, 34 knots
Main Armament:	2 quad SS-N-3 SSM launchers
	1 twin SA-N-1 SAM launcher (GOA)
	2 twin 76mm DP gun mounts

The first of four KYNDA class cruisers appeared in 1962. When introduced, this missile cruiser class was unique in that it carried antiship missiles rather than antiaircraft missiles as the main battery. Antisubmarine rockets and torpedoes are also provided as well as a helicopter landing area (no hangar). The KYNDA is the only Soviet cruiser with reloads for the antiship missile launchers (eight reloads are carried in the superstructure). As in the KRESTA I, JULIETT and ECHO II class submarines, SS-N-3 surface-to-surface cruise missiles carried by this class of ship are estimated to be capable of delivering either a nuclear or high explosive warhead over a distance of about 250nm.

The ships of this class are: ADMIRAL FOKIN, ADMIRAL GOLOVKO, GROZNYY and VARYAG.

SVERDLOV class cruiser

Light Cruiser (CL): SVERDLOV class

Displacement:	17,000 tons full load
Length:	210 meters (693 feet)
Propulsion:	steam turbines, 32 knots
Main Armament:	12 6-inch (152mm) guns
	(4 triple turrets) except
	6 guns in ADMIRAL SENYAVIN and
	9 guns in ZHDANOV and DZERZHINSKIY
	6 twin 100mm guns
	16 twin 37mm guns
	torpedo tubes and mine rails
	SA-N-2 twin SAM launcher in DZERZHINSKIY
	(only ship so equipped)
	SA-N-4 SAM launcher in ADMIRAL SENYAVIN
	and ZHDANOV

Fourteen of these large, light cruisers were built during the early 1950s. (Light cruisers are so designated due to gun size vice ship size, light = guns with less than an 8 inch bore.) Subsequently, one ship was stricken following use as a missile test platform and another was transferred to Indonesia (also later scrapped). In the early 1960s, one SVERDLOV, the DZERZHINSKIY, was converted to a guided missile cruiser (CG). Nine are considered still in commission.

Two SVERDLOVs, the ADMIRAL SENYAVIN and ZHDANOV, were converted to a command ship configuration in the early 1970s. These ships are fitted with staff accommodations and elaborate communications equipment. Some 152-mm guns were removed and helicopter facilities, an SA-N-4 SAM launcher, and several 30-mm antiaircraft guns were installed.

Other ships of this class are: ADMIRAL USHAKOV, ADMIRAL LAZAREV, ALEKSANDR NEVSKIY, ALEKSANDR SUVOROV, DMITRIY POZHARSKIY, MIKHAIL KUTUZOV, MURMANSK, and OKTYABR'SKAYA REVOLUTSIYA.

Guided Missile Destroyer (DDG);
SOVREMENNYY class

Displacement:	7,800 tons full load
Length	159 meters (525 feet)
Propulsion:	steam turbines, 35 knots
Main Armament:	2 quad SS-N-22 missile launchers
	2 single SA-N-7 missile launchers
	2 twin 130mm DP gun mounts
	4 single 30mm Gatling guns
Aircraft:	1 KA-25 HORMONE-B helicopter

This new destroyer design, the lead ship being completed in 1981, is intended for antisurface operations. An expandable hangar is fitted amidships. Series production is underway at the Zhdanov yard in Leningrad, which previously built the KRESTA I/II and KARA cruiser classes. Note the relatively heavy gun armament in these ships.

UDALOY missile destroyer

Guided Missile Destroyer (DDG): UDALOY class

Displacement:	approximately 6,500 tons
Length:	161 meters (531 feet)
Propulsion:	gas turbines, 33-35 knots
Main Armament:	2 quad SS-N-14 ASW missile launchers
	new vertical-launch SA-N-(?) system
	2 single 100mm DP gun mounts
	4 twin 30mm AA gun mounts
Aircraft:	2 KA-27 HELIX ASW helicopters

These are large antisubmarine destroyers. The first ship was completed in 1981 with series production under way. Twin helicopter hangars are fitted aft, with a variable-depth sonar under the flight deck.

Guided Missile Destroyer (DDG): KANIN class

Displacement:	4,750 tons full load
Length:	139 meters (459 feet)
Propulsion:	steam turbines, 35 knots
Main Armament:	1 twin SA-N-1 SAM launcher
	2 quad 57mm AA gun mounts

The KANINs were originally KRUPNYY class guided missile destroyers and were subsequently converted. The KANIN class is primarily an antisubmarine ship with a fair antiaircraft capability. The ship design consists of the basic KRUPNYY destroyer hull and engineering plant armed with antiaircraft guns and missiles, ten antisubmarine torpedo tubes, antisubmarine rocket launchers, and a helicopter platform.

The ships of this class are: BOYKIY, DERZKIY, GNEVNYY, GORDYY, GREMYASHCHIY, UPORNYY, ZHGUCHIY and ZORKIY.

KASHIN guided missile destroyer

Guided Missile Destroyer (DDG): KASHIN/MOD KASHIN classes

Displacement:	4,500 tons full load
Length:	144 meters (475 feet)
Propulsion:	gas turbines, over 35 knots
Main Armament:	2 twin SA-N-1 SAM launchers (GOA)
	4 improved SS-N-2 SSMs (STYX)
	and 4 gatling guns on MOD KASHIN
	2 twin 76mm DP gun mounts

The KASHIN was the world's first large gas-turbine powered warship. The ship's armament consists of two twin antiaircraft missile launchers, dual-purpose guns, five torpedo tubes, mine rails, antisubmarine rockets, and a helicopter landing pad (no hangar). Several ships of the MOD KASHIN class have been provided with improved antiair, antisubmarine, and antiship capabilities over the basic KASHIN class. Additionally, the MOD ships are armed with four launchers for SS-N-2 STYX type missiles and "Gatling" antiaircraft guns. Additional ships will probably be modified. Since the first unit was completed in 1962, 20 ships of the KASHIN class have been built. One KASHIN suffered an internal explosion and sank in the Black Sea in August 1974. Nineteen ships remain in the inventory. The Indian Navy ordered three ships of this class from Soviet shipbuilders to be delivered in the early 1980's.

MOD KILDIN destroyer

Destroyer (DD): MOD KILDIN class

Displacement:	3,500 tons full load
Length:	126 meters (417 feet)
Propulsion:	steam turbines, 34 knots
Main Armament:	4 improved SS-N-2 SSMs
	(STYX) (no reloads)
	2 twin 76mm DP gun mounts
	2 quad 57mm AA gun mounts

Three of the original four KILDIN class destroyers have undergone extensive modification. Their new armament includes four STYX-type missile tubes and two 76-mm twin gun mounts aft in place of the SS-N-1 missile launcher orginally installed. Four torpedo tubes are also provided. These ships were built on a KOTLIN hull plan.

The ships of this class are: NEULOVIMY, BEDOVYY, PROZORLIVY, NEUDERZHIMYY.

Guided Missile Destroyer (DDG): KOTLIN class

Displacement:	3,500 tons full load
Length:	125 meters (413 feet)
Propulsion:	steam turbine, 34 knots
Main Armament:	single twin SA-N-1 SAM launcher
	single twin 130mm DP gun mount
	single quad 45mm AA gun mount

Nine KOTLIN class destroyers were converted to DDGs in the 1960s, with a single twin SA-N-1 SAM launcher installed in place of the after 130-mm mount. These ships retained five of their 21 inch torpedo tubes and have added two 12 barreled (or in two ships 16 barreled) ASW rocket launchers. One unit has had three quad 57-mm mounts and three have had 4 twin 30-mm guns installed. Eight of this class remain in the Soviet inventory, one was transferred to Poland in 1970.

KOTLIN destroyer

Destroyer (DD): KOTLIN class

Displacement:	3,500 tons full load
Length:	126 meters (417 feet)
Propulsion:	steam turbines, 34 knots
Main Armament:	2 twin 130mm DP gun mounts
	2 or 4 twin 25mm gun mounts (MOD KOTLIN)
	4 quad 45mm AA gun mounts
	2 6-barrel ASW rocket launchers (MOD KOTLIN)

Twenty-seven of the fast, general purpose KOTLIN class destroyers were built during the 1950s. Nine of these have since been converted to KOTLIN class DDGs and a number were modernized to MOD KOTLIN status. The MOD version carry 2 or 4 twin 25-mm guns, two 6 barreled ASW rocket launchers and only five 21-inch torpedo tubes. No further conversions or modifications of the remaining standard KOTLIN DDs are anticipated. Although these ships possess heavy conventional and torpedo armament (ten tubes) plus two 12 barreled ASW rocket launchers, they have marginal antisubmarine and antiaircraft capabilities for modern threats. The orginial KOTLIN class DD armament consisted of 2 twin 130-mm guns, 4 quad 45-mm and four 25-mm AA guns, ten torpedo tubes, antisubmarine weapons, and mine rails. Most of the other ships of the class are still in active Soviet service.

SKORYY destroyer

Destroyer (DD): SKORYY class

Displacement:	3,180 tons full load
Length:	121 meters (400 feet)
Propulsion:	steam turbines, 33 knots
Main Armament:	2 twin 130mm DP gun mounts

Seventy-two ships of the SKORYY class were completed from 1949 to 1953. This was the first post-World War II destroyer construction program and are numerically the largest destroyer class built in the Soviet Union. The SKORYY was armed originally with four 5.1-inch guns, two 85-mm AA guns, seven or eight 37-mm AA guns, and ten torpedo tubes plus mine rails, and antisubmarine weapons. The Modified SKORYY configurations received improved antiair and antisubmarine weapons. About 15 SKORYY units remain in service in the Soviet Navy with others in reserve. Although 16 SKORYYs have been transferred to Egypt, Poland, and Indonesia, only some Egyptian units are now active in foreign navies.

KRIVAK missile frigate

Missile Frigate (FFG): KRIVAK I/II class

Displacement:	3,800 tons full load
Length:	123 meters (407 feet)
Propulsion:	gas turbines, 31 knots
Main Armament:	4 SS-N-14 ASW missiles
	2 twin SA-N-4 SAM launchers
	4 76mm AA guns (2 twin mounts) or
	2 100mm DP guns (2 single mounts)
	ASW rockets
	torpedo tubes
	mine rails

The KRIVAK frigates are among the most heavily armed of their type afloat. These are primarily antisubmarine ships with hull-mounted and variable-depth sonars, and ASW missiles, rockets and torpedo tubes. The first KRIVAK put to sea in 1970; a total of 30 units are operational with construction of additional ships continuing. KRIVAK I units have 76-mm dual purpose guns; KRIVAK II—100-mm dual purpose guns.

GRISHA light frigate

Light Frigte (FFL): GRISHA class

Displacement:	1,200 tons full load
Length:	71 meters (236 feet)
Propulsion:	gas turbine/diesel, 30 knots
Main Armament:	GRISHA I—1 twin 57mm AA gun mount,
	1 twin SA-N-4 SAM launcher,
	4 torpedo tubes
	GRISHA II—2 twin 57mm AA gun mounts,
	4 torpedo tubes
	GRISHA III—1 twin 57mm AA gun mount,
	1 twin SA-N-4 SAM launcher,
	1 30mm gatling gun,
	4 torpedo tubes

The three versions of the GRISHA class are primarily designed for coastal antisubmarine operations, but do operate with some regularity with the deployed squadrons on the high seas. The GRISHA II class WFFL is used exclusively by the marine border guards of the KGB. The GRISHA III, with the Gatling gun, has improved close-in air defense. All ships carry two 12-barreled ASW rocket launchers and depth changes as well as a hull-mounted sonar. Some units carry a dipping sonar similar to that used on HORMONE A helicopters. The latter are used with "sprint and drift" tactics, where the ship lay dead on the water while "dipping" (listening on the sonar) then sprints to a new position to "dip" again.

KONI frigate

Frigate (FF): KONI class

Displacement:	2,900 tons full load
Length:	97 meters (320 feet)
Propulsion:	gas turbine/diesel, 28 knots
Main Armament:	1 twin SA-N-4 launcher
	2 twin 76mm dual purpose guns
	2 twin 30mm guns

The KONI class frigate has only been recently introduced. Units have been delivered to Algeria, Cuba, East Germany, and Yugoslavia. Its armament (which also includes ASW rockets and depth charge rails) and sensors are basic with no new technology evident. This class of ship appears to be intended primarily for foreign users, with one ship retained by the Soviet Navy.

Light Frigate (FFL): PETYA I/II classes

Displacement:	1,160 tons full load
Length:	82 meters (270 feet)
Propulsion:	combination diesel/gas turbines, 29 knots
Main Armament:	2 twin 76mm DP gun mounts
	1 five-tube torpedo mounts
	and 2 ASW rocket launchers
	PETYA I has 4 smaller ASW rocket launchers
	and only 1 five-tube torpedo mount

The PETYA class of light frigates is designed primarily for coastal defense, although they operate regularly in the Mediterranean and often in more distant areas. The older PETYA I units became operational in 1960. The improved PETYA II units have two sets of five 16 inch torpedo tubes and two antisubmarine rocket launchers. Some PETYA I's and PETYA II's have been modified to carry variable-depth sonar. About 65 PETYA's have been built, with some units transferred to foreign client states.

MIRKA II light frigate

Light Frigate (FFL): MIRKA I/II classes

Displacement:	1,150 tons full load
Length:	83 meters (272 feet)
Propulsion:	combination diesel/gas turbine, 30 knots
Main Armament:	2 twin 76mm DP gun mounts

The MIRKA class, similar to the PETYA class FFL, is a small fast combatant armed with 76-mm guns, torpedo tubes, and antisubmarine rocket launchers. Nine of about 20 MIRKAs built have two banks of five torpedo tubes and no ASW rocket launchers aft and are designated the MIRKA II class.

RIGA frigate

Frigate (FF): RIGA class

Displacement:	1,510 tons full load
Length:	91 meters (300 feet)
Propulsion:	diesels, 28 knots
Main Armament:	3 single 100mm DP gun mounts
	2 twin 37mm AA gun mounts
	1 three-tube torpedo mount

An estimated 64 RIGA class frigates were built from 1952 through 1958. The approximately 35 units still active in the Soviet Navy have been given improved antisubmarine capabilities with the addition of ASW rocket launchers. Ships of this class have been transferred to Bulgaria, East Germany, Finland, and Indonesia.

117

SMALL COMBATANTS

NANUCHKA I guided missile patrol combatant

Guided Missile Patrol Combatant (PGG): NANUCHKA I/II classes

Displacement:	770 tons full load
Length:	59 meters (196 feet)
Propulsion:	diesels, over 30 knots
Main Armament:	6 SS-N-9 SSMs
	1 twin SA-N-4 SAM launcher
	single twin 57mm AA guns
	(NANUCHKA I)
	single 76mm AA gun
	1 30mm Gatling Gun
	(NANUCHKA III)

The NANUCHKA I and III classes are the largest of the Soviet guided missile patrol combatants. The class was designed for improved endurance and better sea-keeping qualties than earlier missile craft. The NANUCHKA armament includes six SS-N-9 antiship cruise missiles with a range of about 60 nautical miles. Significant defensive weapons are also provided. The first NANUCHKA was completed in 1969; construction continues. The NANUCHKA II class, equipped with four SS-N-2 missiles, is the export version and has been delivered to India.

Missile Attack Boat (PTG): OSA I/II class

Displacement:	240 tons full load
Length:	39 meters (128 feet)
Propulsion:	diesels, 34 knots
Main Armament:	4 SS-N-2 STYX SSMs
	2 twin 30mm gun mounts

The OSA is numerically, the largest class of missile attack boat in the Soviet navy with some 40 OSA I/II units currently in inventory. OSA class missile boats are large follow-ons to the obsolete KOMARs. OSAs are fitted with four STYX-type (SS-N-2) antiship cruise missile tubes plus 30-mm AA guns. Indian-manned OSAs sank one Pakistani destroyer and severely damaged a second in the 1971 Indo-Pakistani War. They were also thought responsible for the sinking of several merchant ships. Over 100 of the OSA class missile boats have been transferred to other countries, including Bulgaria, China (PRC), Cuba, Egypt, Algeria, Libya, East Germany, India, Poland, Romania, Syria, Yugoslavia, Iraq, Finland, Algeria, Bulgaria, North Korea, and Somalia. The OSA II units have an improved, longer range SS-N-2 missile.

AMPHIBIOUS SHIPS

IVAN ROGOV amphibious assault transport dock

Amphibious Assault Transport Dock (LPD): IVAN ROGOV class

Displacement:	13,000 tons full load
Length:	158 meters (522 feet)
Propulsion:	gas turbine, about 20 knots
Main Armament:	1 twin 76mm DP gun mount
	1 twin SA-N-4 SAM launcher
	4 single 30mm Gatling guns
	1 122mm multiple rocket launcher

With the introduction of the IVAN ROGOV LPD in 1978, the Soviet Navy gained two new capabilities for its amphibious assault forces. First, the ROGOV has a floodable well deck that is intended to carry air cushion vehicles as well as conventional landing craft. The LEBED class medium landing craft (air cushion) (LCMA) vehicle has been deployed with ROGOV. A total of three can be carried in the well. Additionally, the ROGOV has a helicopter hangar and two landing decks. To date, the HORMONE is the only helicopter observed operating from ROGOV. It is estimated that IVAN ROGOV can lift a Soviet naval infantry battalion reinforced with one company of tanks and other combat support equipment or a total of approximately 550 troops, 30 armored personnel carriers, and 10 tanks. Included are bow doors and ramp for over the beach off loading as well as a roll-on/roll-off capability onto the weather deck and the tank decks forward of the well. This ship is by far the largest amphibious unit to join the Soviet Navy. Only two ships have been built.

ALLIGATOR amphibious vehicle landing ship

Amphibious Vehicle Landing Ship (LST): ALLIGATOR class

Displacement: 4,700 tons full load
Length: 113 meters (372 feet)
Propulsion: diesels, 16 knots
Main Armament: single twin 57mm gun mount
                      single twin arm shore bombardment
                      rocket launcher (some units)

The ALLIGATOR is a landing ship with a tank deck and bow doors as well as a stern ramp. LSTs are used to transport Naval Infantry units with their equipment and vehicles. These ships are used regularly on distant deployments to the Mediterranean, Indian Ocean and West Africa. Armament varies on a number of these ships. Some have 2 AS-N-5 quad SAM launchers; two have 2 twin 25-mm AA guns and several have 40 tube 122-mm shore bombardment rocket launchers. Fourteen of this class were built before production closed.

ROPUCHA amphibious vehicle landing ship

Amphibious Vehicle Landing Ship (LST): ROPUCHA class

Displacement: 3,200 tons full load
Length: 113 meters (373 feet)
Propulsion: diesels, 16 knots
Main Armament: 2 twin 57mm gun mounts
                      some have 2 SA-N-5 quad SAM launchers

The Polish built ROPUCHA class LSTs have a covered vehicle deck with both bow and stern doors. The newest of Soviet LSTs, it was designed to carry a balanced load of troops and vehicles. Like the ALLIGATORs, ships of this class often deploy with the Soviet Mediterranean, West African, and Indian Ocean Squadrons. The Soviets recently transferred one of these ships to the navy of South Yemen. About 11 remain in the Soviet order-of-battle.

121

Medium Amphibious Assault Landing Ship (LSM): POLNOCNY class

Displacement:	770 to 1,150 tons full load
Length:	73 to 81 meters (241-268 feet)
Propulsion:	diesels, 18 knots
Main Armament:	1 or 2 twin 30mm gun mounts
	2 18-tube 140mm shore bombardment
	rocket launchers
	some have 4 SA-N-5 quad SAM launchers

The POLNOCNYs are Polish-built medium landing ships with bow doors and a covered vehicle deck. They have been built in three variants, each of different length and displacement. About 50 ships are currently in the Soviet Navy with more than 20 in the Polish Navy. Other units have been transferred to Algeria, Egypt, Indonesia, India, Iraq, Somalia and South Yemen. Several variations exist within the general POLNOCNY class with different bridge configurations, armament, and payloads. Most ships are armed with 30-mm AA guns and multi-barrel shore bombardment rocket launchers.

Appendix D. SOVIET AIRCRAFT DESCRIPTIONS

The combat capabilities of Naval Aviation are one of the main indicators of the striking power of our modern Navy. Naval Aviation has become truly oceanic in nature, and it has been transformed into a most important naval warfare resource.

Admiral of the Fleet of the Soviet Union
S.G. GORSHKOV

This appendix provides basic descriptive data and photographs of the more significant Soviet Naval aircraft. Naval aviation comprises about eleven percent of the total Soviet combat aircraft inventory. It has become a significant adjunct to the expanding Soviet Naval structure. The fact that naval aviation is receiving the new supersonic BACKFIRE bomber at about the same rate as the Soviet Air Force, and the growing carrier based elements, attests to the relative high priority Soviet Naval aviation is receiving.

Arrangement: Aircraft are arranged alphabetically by NATO code name.

Classification: The dimensions, characteristics, and general information contained in the appendix are approximate.

Designations: All aircraft names given in this appendix are NATO code names: "B" names prefix Bomber aircraft; "F" names prefix Fighter aircraft; "M" names prefix Miscellaneous aircraft, including maritime resonnaissance/patrol aircraft; and "H" names prefix Helicopters. One-syllable names denote propeller driven aircraft and two-syllable names are used for jet aircraft. The Soviet designation scheme, which uses letters derived from the name(s) of the aircraft designer (e.g., MIG, TU, KA) and sequential numbers, provides a universal designation basis for Soviet aircraft.

In English we refer to the naval air arm as Soviet Naval Aviation (SNA). In Russian it is called AVIATSIYA VOYENNO-MORSKOGO FLOTA (AVMF).

FORGER VTOL fighter-attack aircraft with APHID AA-8 missiles

STRIKE/BOMBER AIRCRAFT

BACKFIRE strike aircraft

BACKFIRE

Length:	40 meters (132 feet)
Wingspan:	swept, 26 meters (86 feet)
	extended, 34 meters (113 feet)
Gross Weight:	270,000 lbs.
Engines:	2 turbofan
Maximum Speed:	approx. 1,100 knots

Almost 100 operational model BACKFIRE B aircraft are deployed in Soviet Naval Aviation. They can carry air-to-surface cruise missiles of the AS-4 type. The role for these supersonic variable-geometry (swing) wing bombers in SNA is missile strike against carrier task forces and similar high value targets as well as bombing and mining tasks. As additional aircraft are produced, reconnaissance and electronic warfare may be added missions of their roles. BACKFIREs, flown by Soviet Long-Range Aviation, are equipped with a tail turret (probably twin 23-mm guns). Some have been reported with external weapons racks for carrying mines or bombs. Although not counted under any SALT Treaty, the Soviets have agreed to limit production of this aircraft to a total of 30 per year in a related separate agreement.

BACKFIRE strike aircraft with KITCHEN AS-4 missile

124

TU-16 BADGER

Length:	37 meters (120 feet)
Wingspan:	35 meters (113 feet)
Gross Weight:	115,000 lbs.
Engines:	2 turbojets
Maximum Speed:	540 knots

The BADGER TU-16 twin-turbojet medium bomber is employed by Soviet Naval Aviation in antiship, reconnaissance, electronic warfare, and tanker roles. the BADGER is the most numerous aircraft type in Soviet Naval Aviation with currently over 400 in service. The early versions of this aircraft first entered naval service in the late 1950s, and the design has been extensively developed since that time. BADGER-C and -G variants are armed with stand-off missiles for antiship strike; one AS-2 or two AS-4 on the former and two AS-5 or AS-4 on the latter. BADGER A bombers, which carry up to 9 tons of gravity (free-fall) bombs, are probably employed primarily for training and mine laying. About 70 BADGER-A aircraft are configured as tankers for in-flight refueling of strike and reconnaissance aircraft. About 75 BADGERs are employed as specially configured reconnaissance and electronic variants. BADGERs also are flown by Soviet Long-Range Aviation and the air arms of China (PRC), Egypt, Indonesia, and Iraq. Most BADGERs have two or three twin 23-mm gun turrets.

TU-20 BEAR D

Length:	48 meters (156 feet)
Wingspan:	49 meters (159 feet)
Gross Weight:	356,000 lbs.
Engines:	4 turboprop (counter-rotating propellers)
Maximum Speed:	450 knots

The TU-20 BEARs are the largest Soviet Naval Aircraft. About 50 of the Bear D variant are flown in the maritime surveillance/reconnaissance role. As an assist in resolving over-the-horizon targeting, high flying BEAR Ds can provide cruise missile guidance information to aircraft, surface ship, and submarine launch platforms. The BEAR D has an unrefueled range of approximately 15,000 kilometers (8,000 nautical miles). Naval BEARs have flown from bases in the Murmansk area around the North Cape, down the Norwegian Sea, and across the Atlantic Ocean, landing in Cuba or Guinea. BEAR Ds have also been deployed to Somalia, Angola, and Vietnam, with some having flown reconnaissance missions along the U.S. east coast. BEAR A, B, C, and E variants (The latter is a reconnaissance version) are flown by Soviet Long-Range Aviation. The BEAR B and C carry the AS-3 KANGAROO missile, which is capable of attacking sea targets and are occasionally exercised in maritime strike roles. Most BEARs are equipped with three twin 23-mm guns. The BEAR F is the naval antisubmarine warfare variant. TU-95 is the Tupolev bureau designation.

TU-20 BEAR F

Length:	49 meters (162 feet)
Wingspan:	51 meters (168 feet)
Gross Weight:	380,000 lbs.
Engines:	4 turboprop
Maximum Speed:	450 knots

The BEAR F is the Soviet's long range antisubmarine warfare aircraft. This variant of the BEAR entered service prior to 1973 and is suited primarily for long range, antisubmarine warfare and open-ocean maritime operations. The aircraft's equipment includes sonobuoys, radar for submarine detection, and torpedoes and depth bombs for attack. BEAR Fs continue to enter the naval aviation inventory. TU-142 is the design bureau designation.

BLINDER medium bomber

TU-22 BLINDER

Length:	42 meters (137 feet)
Wingspan:	29 meters (95 feet)
Gross Weight:	185,000 lbs.
Engines:	2 turbojets
Maximum Speed:	1,000 knots

The TU-22 BLINDER twin-turbojet medium bomber is employed by the Soviet Navy in both attack and reconnaissance roles. There are about 50 BLINDER A aircraft in naval service which carry gravity bombs. A few BLINDER Cs are configured for reconnaissance. Armament includes a twin 23-mm gun tail turret. These aircraft have a supersonic dash capability. BLINDERs, including the BLINDER B, the AS-4 KITCHEN missile variant, are also flown by Soviet Long-Range Aviation as well as the air forces of Iraq and Libya.

FORGER VTOL fighter/attack aircraft

YAK-36 FORGER

Length:	15 meters (49 feet)
Wingspan:	7 meters (23 feet)
Gross Weight:	22,000 lbs.
Engines:	2 lift-only jets and
	1 lift/cruise jet
Maximum Speed:	transonic

The YAK-36 FORGER is a VTOL (Vertical Take-Off and Landing) aircraft first deployed in mid-1976 on the Soviet carrier KIEV. The aircraft uses both the lift-only and the lift/cruise engines in vertical flight and while transitioning into horizontal flight. The lift-only engines are shut down during normal flight. The FORGER's four wing stations are believed to be capable of mounting a variety of weapons including air-to-air missiles, rocket pods, machine guns, bombs, and tactical air-to-surface missiles, as well as auxiliary fuel tanks. While the exact role of FORGER A is unclear, it appears suitable for a wide range of missions such as air defense, close air support, reconnaissance, and antiship strike. The FORGER B is a two-seat (combat capable) trainer version of the FORGER. Although the FORGER's capabilities are less than most Western contemporary aircraft, it gives the Soviets a fixed-wing sea-based air capability where they had none before. New, more advanced ship-borne aircraft types will appear in the Soviet fleet during the 1980s.

FITTER fighter/attack aircraft

SU-17 FITTER

Length:	18 meters (58 feet)
Wingspan:	swept, 10.5 meters (34.5 feet)
	extended, 14 meters (45 feet)
Gross Weight:	37,500 lbs.
Engines:	1 turbojet
Maximum Speed:	720 knots

This variable-geometry-wing aircraft is primarily a ground support fighter. It is flown by the Soviet Air Forces as well as the Navy, with the latter having FITTER C/D units in the Baltic and Pacific Fleets. It is a single-seat aircraft with two fixed 30mm cannon and six or eight stores stations for a variety of weapons or drop tanks.

HAZE A antisubmarine helicopter

MI-14 HAZE A

Length (fuselage):	11 meters (60 feet)
Rotor Diameter:	21 meters (70 feet)
Gross Weight:	24,000 lbs.
Engines:	2 turboshaft jets
Maximum Speed:	135 knots

The HAZE A, an antisubmarine warfare helicopter, was adapted from the twin turbine MI-8 HIP transport helicopter including the adaption of the fuselage to a boat hull. The rotary wing aircraft has been observed with towed Magnetic Anomaly Detection and dipping sonar and has been operational since 1975. Over 50 of these new helicopters are believed to have entered operational service in the SNA. The HAZE A is the replacement for the shore-based HOUND ASW helicopters. In its present configuration, the HAZE is not suitable for regular operation from ships as its rotors and tail cannot be folded to facilitate storage. The HAZE is also in service with other Warsaw Pact countries.

HORMONE helicopter

KA-25 HORMONE

Length (fuselage):	10 meters (32 feet)
Rotor Diameter:	16 meters (52 feet)
Gross Weight:	16,000 lbs.
Engines:	2 turboshafts (counter-rotating main rotors)
Maximum Speed:	130 knots

The HORMONE is the Soviet Navy's standard shipboard helicopter. It is embarked in the KRESTA I and II, and KARA classes of missile cruisers, the MOSKVA and KIEV classes of aviation ships, the IVAN ROGOV class landing ship, the BEREZINA class replenishment ship, and most, if not all, the four new warship classes. The helicopters are configured for antisubmarine warfare (HORMONE A), missile targeting (HORMONE B), or for utility functions (HORMONE C). HORMONE B helicopters are embarked in ships with antiship cruise missiles. About 200 HORMONEs are currently active in the Soviet Navy. Distinctive features of ungainly looking helicopter are a chin-mounted radome, triple tails, and two counter-rotating rotors. The HORMONE A has an internal weapons bay for torpedoes or depth charges and carries sonobuoys, dipping sonar, and an optical sensor. The HORMONE C has several variations including search and rescue, and transport and vertical replenishment.

HELIX antisubmarine helicopter on destroyer UDALOY

KA-27 HELIX

Length:	12 meters (39.5 feet)
Rotor Diameter:	17 meters (55 feet)
Gross Weight:	
Engines:	2 turboshafts
Maximum Speed:	

The HELIX is a successor to the HORMONE, which it strongly resembles. So far it has appeared only in an ASW configuration for use aboard ASW surface combatants and aircraft carriers.

130

BE-12 MAIL

Length:	30 meters (99 feet)
Wingspan:	29 meters (97 feet)
Gross Weight:	65,000 lbs.
Engines:	2 turboprops
Maximum Speed:	330 knots

Soviet Naval Aviation operates these amphibious aircraft in maritime reconnaissance and antisubmarine warfare roles. The MAIL has distinctive gull-shaped wings, an elongated radar dome nose, and a MAD antenna protruding from the tail. Its weapons are carried on underwing pylons and in a weapons bay in the after section of the hull. Torpedoes, mines, or depth charges can be carried.

IL-38 MAY

Length:	37 meters (130 feet)
Wingspan:	37 meters (123 feet)
Gross Weight:	141,000 lbs.
Engines:	4 turboprops
Cruise Speed:	340 knots

Entering service in 1968, the MAY is used primarily for open ocean patrol and antisubmarine warfare. The aircraft was adapted from a commercial aircraft design (the IL-18 COOT) in the same manner that the U.S. Navy P-3 ORION was developed from the commercial ELECTRA aircraft. It closely resembles the P-3. The MAY has a radome under the forward fuselage and a MAD antenna protruding from the tail. ASW torpedoes are carried in an internal weapons bay. The Soviet aircraft has expendable sonobuoys and nonacoustic sensors, as well as a computerized tactical evaluation capability. Endurance is reported to be 12 hours at a patrol speed of about 220 knots. These aircraft have been deployed outside the Soviet Union on a number of occasions over the last several years, mainly to Aden, where they flew surveillance on U.S. naval forces operating in the Arabian Sea. MAYs are also flown by the Indian Air Force. This type does not appear to be under construction any longer.

Appendix E. MISSILE GUIDE

Air-to-Surface Missile	NATO Code Name	Range	Platforms
AS-2	KIPPER	About 100nm	BADGER C/G
AS-3	KANGAROO	200–300nm	BEAR B/C
AS-4	KITCHEN	150-250nm	BLINDER B, BACKFIRE, BADGER C/G
AS-5	KELT	About 100nm	BADGER G
AS-6	KINGFISH	150-250nm	BADGER C/G

Surface-to-Air			
SA-N-1		About 10nm	KRESTA I, KYNDA, KANIN, KASHIN, KOTLIN
SA-N-2		About 30nm	DZERZHINSKIY (SVERDLOV class)
SA-N-3		About 30nm	KIEV, MOSKVA, KARA, KRESTA II
SA-N-4		About 8nm	KIEV, KARA, KIROV, SVERDLOV, KONI, GRISHA I/III, KRIVAK I/II, NANUCHKA, SARANCHA, IVAN ROGOV, BEREZINA
SA-N-5		About 3nm	ROPUCHA, POLNOCNY, some AGIs
SA-N-6		About 30nm	KIROV
SA-N-7			SOVREMENNYY

Surface (or Sub-Surface) -to-Surface (or Sub-Surface)			
SS-N-1	SCRUBBER	About 100nm	KILDEN, KRUPNYY
SS-N-2	STYX	About 25nm (SSM)	OSA I, KOMAR, NANUCHKA II, OSA I
SS-N-2 (Imp)	STYX (Improved)	About 40nm (SSM)	OSA II, MOD KASHIN, MOD KILDEN, MATKA, TARANTUL
SS-N-3b	SEPAL	About 250nm	KRESTA I, KYNDA,
SS-N-3c	SHADDOCK	(SSM)	ECHO I/II, JULIETT, WHISKEY Conversion
SS-N-4	SARK	About 350nm (SLBM)	GOLF, HOTEL, ZULU V
SS-N-5	SERB	About 700nm (SLBM	GOLF II, HOTEL II
SS-N-6	SAWFLY	1600nm (SLBM)	GOLF IV (Test Platform), YANKEE I

Missile	NATO Code Name	Range/Type	Platforms
SS-N-7		About 30nm (SSM)	CHARLIE I
SS-N-8		4000nm + (SLBM)	DELTA I/II, GOLF III (Test Platform)
SS-N-9	SIREN	About 60nm (SSM)	NANUCHKA, SARANCHA, CHARLIE II, PAPA
SS-N-10	cancelled designator		
SS-N-11	cancelled designator		
SS-N-12		About 300nm (SSM)	KIEV, ECHO II
SS-NX-13		(SLBM)	Experimental, inactive
SS-N-14	SILEX	About 25nm (ASW)	KARA, KIROV, KRESTA II, KRIVAK I/II, UDALOY
SS-N-15		Short Range (ASW)	Newer classes of submarines
SS-NX-16		Short Range (ASW)	Newer classes of submarines
SS-N-17		1600nm + (SLBM)	YANKEE II
SS-N-18		About 5000nm (SLBM)	DELTA III
SS-N-19		Over 250nm	OSCAR, KIROV
SS-N-20		Over 4000nm	TYPHOON, GOLF V (Test Platform)
SS-N-21		1,860mm	Submarines (Torpedo Tubes)
SS-N-22		Long-range Cruise Missile	SOVREMENNYY
SUW-N-1		Short (ASW)	KIEV, MOSKVA

A Soviet intelligence collector (AGI) closes on the stern of a U.S. aircraft carrier while observing flight operations in the Mediterranean Sea. Some of the larger Soviet AGIs are armed.

GLOSSARY

NOTE: Definition of larger ship type designators such as SSBN, SS, CG, DDG, FEL, CVHG, LSM, LPD, etc. may be found in Appendix B and Appendix C.

AAW	Antiair Warfare
AGI	Intelligence collection ship
AOR	Replenishment oiler
AS-(number)	U.S. designation for Soviet air-to-surface missile (see App. E)
ASUW	Antisurface Warfare
ASW	Antisubmarine Warfare
C^3	Command, Control and Communications
CINC	Commander-in-Chief
CTOL	Conventional Take-Off and Landing (aircraft)
ELINT	Electronic Intelligence
Gatling gun	a generic term for a multibarrel machine gun
ICBM	Intercontinental Ballistic Missile
MIRV	Multiple Independently Targeted Re-entry Vehicle
mm	millimeters
MRV	Multiple Re-entry Vehicle
NATO	North Atlantic Treaty Organization
nm	nautical miles (equals 6,079.115 ft.)
PCS	submarine chaser
PCSH	Submarine chaser (Hydrofoil)
PG	Gunboat
PTH	Torpedo boat (Hydrofoil)
PTL	Small Torpedo boat
RO/RO	Roll-on/Roll-off
SA-N-(number)	U.S. designation for Soviet naval surface-to-air missile (see App. E)
SAM	Surface-to-Air Missile
SESS	Space Event Support Ship
SLBM	Submarine-Launched Ballistic Missile
SLOC	Sea Lines of communication
SNA	Soviet Naval Aviation
SS-N-(number)	U.S. designation for Soviet naval surface-to-surface or submarine-to-surface missile (see App. E)
VSTOL	Vertical and Short Take-Off and Landing (aircraft)
VTOL	Vertical Take-Off and Landing (aircraft)
WIG	Wing-in-ground effect (aircraft)

Index

O

OHIO-class submarine, 8, 10, 41
Oiler-store class ship; BEREZINA, 27, 44, **45**, 79, 130
Out-of-area ship days, 16
OKEAN fleet exercises, 7, 25, 28, 46
Order of battle, Soviet Navy, 85-86
OSA-class missile boat, 4, **9**, 37, 38, 47, **119**
OSCAR-class submarine, 40, 41, 77, 79, **96**

P

P-3 ORION aircraft, 43, 132
PAPA-class submarine, **97**
Pacific Ocean Fleet, 20, 28, 76, 77, 78
Pacific Ocean-Soviet deployment, 21
Patrol escort class ships; POTI, 47
Personnel, Soviet Naval, 51-59; Enlisted men, 52, 54-55; Leadership, 58-59; Officers, 55-58; Pre-service Training, 51-52; Political action, 59
Peter I, Tsar, 3
PETYA-class frigate, 37, 54, **116**
POLARIS-class submarine, 4
POLNOCNY-class amphibious ship, 44, 47, 80, **122**
POSEIDON-class submarine, 5
POTI-class patrol escort, 47
PRIMORYE-class intelligence collection ship, 46
PUEBLO-intelligence gathering ship, 46

R

Rank and Grades-Soviet Navy, 54-58
REGULUS cruise missile program, U.S., 40
Replenishment class ships, **23**, **24**, 27, 44, **45**, **76**, 79, 130
RETVIZAN, Tsarist battleship, **2**
RIGA-class frigate, 37, 47, **117**
ROMEO-class submarine, 18, 95, **97**
ROPHUCHA-class amphibious ship, 44, 79, **121**
RO/RO ship, **62**, **64**
RUSSIA-Soviet liner, **60**
Russo-Japanese War, 1904, 3

S

SALT I, treaty, 41, 75, 101, 124
SARANCHA-class hydrofoil, 38
SASHA-class minesweeper, 38
Satellites, ELINT, 46
Schools-Soviet naval, 53
Sea-Lines of Communication Interdiction, Soviet, 10
Sea Power of the State, 7, 28
Shapiro, William, 26
Shield '82 wargames, 80
Ship descriptions, Soviet, 87-122
Ships-Naval Force Levels, U.S.-U.S.S.R., 72
Shipyards, Soviet, 24, 68-69, 75, 78, 79
SKORYY-class destroyers, 36, **113**
SLAVA-class cruiser, 35, **105**
Smirnov, N. I., 58
SONYA-class minesweeper, 38
Soviet Military Encyclopedia, 7
Soviet Naval Headquarters, 25
SOVIET UNION, battleship, **4**
Soviet State policy, Naval support of, 11, 13
SOVREMENNYY-class antisurface destroyer, 22, **36**, 37, 77, 78, 79, **109**
Space events support ships; KOSMONAUT VLADI-MIR KOMAROV, **68**; KOSMONAUT YURI

GAGARIN, **67**
Stalin, Joseph, 3, 4
STALINGRAD-class cruiser, 4
Strategic warfare, Soviet, offensive, 8-10
Submarine chaser-class ship; BABOUCHKA, 38
Submarines, U.S., GEORGE WASHINGTON, 4; HOLLAND, **2**; LOS ANGELES class, 41; OHIO, 8, 9, 10, 41; TRIDENT class, 5, 24, 41, 75
Submarines-U.S.S.R., ALFA, 37, 41, **70**, 77, 79, **88**; BRAVO, **88**; CHARLIE, 39, 40, 76, **89**; DELTA, 8, 16, 41, 75, 79, **90**, 91, 101; ECHO, 37, 40, **91**, **92**, 108; FOXTROT, 18, 19, 24, 37, 41, 80, 81, **92**; GOLF, 10, 11, 19, 41, 46, **93**; HOTEL, 10, 41, 64, 75, **94**; INDIA, **94**; JULIETT, **95**, 108; KILO, 37, 76, 77, 95; LIMA, **95**; NOVEMBER, 37, **96**; OSCAR, 40, 41, 77, 79, **96**; PAPA, **97**; ROMEO, 18, 95, **97**; TANGO, 24, 37, 41, 77, **98**; TYPHOON, 8, 16, 26, 41, 75, 79, 82, **98**, 101; VICTOR, 41, 76, **99-100**; WHISKEY, 18, 95, 97, **99**; YANKEE, 8, 9, **40**, 41, 75, **101**; ZULU, **101**
SUBROC missile, U.S., 24
Suez Canal, 18-19, 20
Suez invasion-1958, 6
SVERDLOV-class light cruiser, 4, 5, 11, 35, 46, **48**, **75**, **108**

T

TANGO-class submarine, 24, 37, 41, 77, **98**
TARANTUL-class gunboat, 38
Tatu, Michael, 29
TICONDEROGA-class destroyer, 35
TOMAHAWK, cruise missile, U.S., 23, 24, 79
Training, Soviet Naval, 52, 53
TRIDENT-class submarine, 5, 10, 24, 41
Turkish Straits, 11, 19, 27, n31
TURYA-class hydrofoil, **38**
TYPHOON-class submarine, 8, 16, 26, 41, 75, 79, 82, **98**, 101

U

UDALOY-class ASW destroyer, 10, 22, **27**, 36, 77, 78, **109**, **130**

V

VANYA-class minesweeper, 38
VICTOR-class submarine, 37, 41, 76, **99-100**
Vladivostok, 76, 91
VYTEGRALES-class cargo ship, **12**

W

Watkins, James D., 82
West African Squadron-Soviet, 20
Wheelus Air Force Base, 6
WHISKEY-class submarine, 18, 47, 95, 97, **100**
White Sea, 24, 68
Wing-In-Ground (WIG) effect vehicle, 25
WICHITA, 45
World War I & II, 3

Y

YANKEE-class submarine, 8, 9, **40**, 41, 75, **101**
YURKA-class ocean minesweepers, 38

Z

ZULU-class submarine, **101**